For Edward,
always and again

# LEAVING CHURCH

# LEAVING CHURCH

## A Memoir of Faith

BARBARA BROWN TAYLOR

HarperSanFrancisco
*A Division of HarperCollinsPublishers*

Portions of this book have appeared previously in different form in *The Christian Century* (excerpts from "The Sacred Well," August 2–9, 2000, and "Beyond Belief," January 13, 2004); "The Vocation of Being Human," in *Explorations in Theology and Vocation*, ed. William E. Rogers (Greenville, SC: Furman University Center for Theological Exploration of Vocation, 2005); "Friends of the Disciples" in *Preaching in the New Millennium*, ed. Frederick J. Streets (Yale University Press, 2005); "Way Beyond Belief" in *Shouts & Whispers*, ed. Jennifer L. Holberg (Wm. B. Eerdmans Publishing Company, 2006); and "Listening to the Nos" in *Pastoral Psychology* 52, no. 1–2 (November 2003): 163–171, © 2003 by Human Sciences Press, Inc., with kind permission of Spring Science and Business Media.

Scripture from the New Revised Standard Version of the Bible, copyright ©1989, Division of Christian Education of the National Council of the Churches of Christ in the United States of America

HarperCollins books may be purchased for educational, business, or sales promotional use. For information please write: Special Markets Department, Harper-Collins Publishers, 10 East 53rd Street, New York, NY 10022.

HarperCollins Web site: http://www.harpercollins.com
HarperCollins®, 📖®, and HarperSanFrancisco™ are
trademarks of HarperCollins Publishers

FIRST EDITION
*Designed by Joseph Rutt*

Library of Congress Cataloging-in-Publication Data.

Taylor, Barbara Brown.
Leaving church : a memoir of faith /Barbara Brown Taylor.— 1st ed.
p. cm.
1. Taylor, Barbara Brown. 2. Episcopal Church — Clergy — Biography.
3. Anglican Communion — United States — Clergy — Biography.
I. Title.

ISBN-10: 0–06–77174–7
ISBN-13: 978–0–06–077174–4

06 07 08 09 10 RRD(H) 10 9 8 7 6 5 4 3 2 1

# Contents

# Introduction

Because I am looking at the Special Events page of my calendar, I know that I was ordained in the Episcopal Church twenty years ago last May. If the event had been a marriage instead of an ordination, then that would have been my china anniversary, with silver just five years away. I might have looked forward to receiving a new serving platter or soup tureen in my wedding pattern from my old sweetheart—or, if he forgot, to buying some replacement pieces myself so that I could finally let the cracked ones go. Anniversaries that end in zeros merit some sort of ceremony, no matter what they mark, and I had meant to do justice by this one. Twenty years of priesthood was a lot to reflect upon, especially for someone who no longer spent every Sunday in church. I had fully intended to hallow the day by going to a monastery for the weekend or at least spending a couple of hours in contemplative prayer. Instead, the date slipped right past me. All these months later, I am trying hard to remember how I spent it.

Since May is graduation month, perhaps I spent the day sitting on a folding chair on the basketball court at the college where I now teach, watching another class of giddy graduates receive their diplomas. Or since May is the month when the lush spring fescue becomes safe for horses to eat, perhaps I spent the day checking the fence line of the summer pasture before turning my two quarter horses out in it. Since I feed the chickens every day, I believe I can safely say that I marked the anniversary of my ordination by throwing a can of scratch grains to two Rhode Island Red hens and two Dominiques before taking four brown eggs from their communal nest.

The truth is that while I have never felt more engaged in what I was ordained to do, few of my initial expectations have been met. By now I expected to be a seasoned parish minister, wearing black clergy shirts grown gray from frequent washing. I expected to love the children who hung on my legs after Sunday morning services until they grew up and had children of their own. I expected to spend the rest of my life writing sermons, leading worship, delivering pastoral care to the living, and burying the dead—not for twenty years but for all my years. I even expected to be buried wearing the same red vestments in which I was ordained.

Today those vestments are hanging in the sacristy of an Anglican church in Kenya, my church pension is frozen, and I am as likely to spend Sunday mornings with friendly Quakers, Presbyterians, or Congregationalists as I am with the Episcopalians who remain my closest kin. Sometimes I even keep the Sabbath with a cup of steaming Assam tea on my front porch, watching towhees vie for the highest perch in the poplar tree while God watches me. These days I earn my living teaching school, not leading worship, and while I still dream of opening a small restaurant in Clarkesville or volunteering at an eye clinic in Nepal, there is no guarantee that I will not run off with the circus before I am through. This is not the life I planned or the life I recommend to others. But it is the life that has turned out to be mine, and the central revelation in it for me — that the call to serve God is first and last the call to be fully human — seems important enough to witness to on paper. This book is my attempt to do that.

Like every believer I know, my search for real life has led me through at least three distinct seasons of faith, not once or twice but over and over again. Jesus called them finding life, losing life, and finding life again, with the paradoxical promise that finders will be losers while those who lose their lives for his sake will wind up finding them again. In Greek the word is *psyche,* meaning not only "life" but also the conscious self, the personality, the soul. You do not have to die in order to discover the truth of this teaching, in other words. You only need to lose track of who you are, or who you thought you were supposed to be, so that you end up lying flat on the dirt floor basement of your heart. Do this, Jesus says, and you will live.

As hard as preachers may work to clarify this koan, I do not believe that it can be done. The promise contains truth that can only be experienced, and even when it is I do not know anyone who readily volunteers for loss again. Yet loss is how we come to surrender our lives — if not to God, then at least to the Great Beyond — and even those who profess no faith in anything but the sap that makes the green blade rise may still confess that losing really has helped them find their ways again. My losses have been modest compared to most. I am an educated, middle-class white woman who has never so much as broken a bone. I have been married twice, once not so well and now well for more than twenty years. The suffering of children has broken my heart, but none of those children has been my own. I have buried one parent but still enjoy the company of the other, and my two younger sisters and their families are all alive and well.

I guess you could say that my losses have been chiefly in the area of faith, and specifically in the area of being certain who God is, what God wants of me, and what it means to be Christian in a world where religion often seems to do more harm than good. When I was ordained twenty years ago, I was far surer of those things than I am now—so sure that I decided to spend my life helping other people become more sure of them too. Some of those people clearly humored me, since they knew far more about the life of faith than I did, but others seemed genuinely grateful for my ministrations.

Together we explored the mysteries of holy baptism and communion along with the vast and varied books of the Bible. Together we navigated both the predictable passages of human life on earth and some of its more unusual cruelties, taking comfort in the cycle of the church year, which never led us into the pit without lighting a way out again. Together we even managed to overcome our preoccupation with our own needs long enough to tend the needs of our neighbors, although never without the strong temptation to congratulate ourselves for our good works.

Like most ordained women in those days, I served as an associate on a large church staff, working under the supervision of an ordained man who helped shape my desire to be the priest in charge one day. I am not sure I can defend that ambition now, except to say that it seemed the natural course of things. Does anyone ride in a car without wanting one day to steer it? I wanted one day to lead a congregation of my own — to guide a course, shape a vision, serve a people, make a difference. I wanted to see what I could do with a church of my own. Although the hubris in that admission now causes me to wince, I suppose it was no worse than that of any bride laying up her trousseau. I wanted to spend the rest of my life as close to God as I could get, and full-time parish ministry seemed to offer me the best chance of doing that.

In the tenth year of my priesthood, I found what I was looking for. A small, historical parish in north Georgia with a reputation for taking risks began looking for a new rector. When my husband Ed and I visited, it was love at first sight. After a lengthy courtship, I discovered that the church I wanted also wanted me. I was about to go and do what I believed God was calling me to go and do, without the least suspicion that finding my life might involve losing it — or that loss, in the end, might be cause for praise.

# LEAVING
# CHURCH

PART ONE

# Finding

*The only thing worth writing about is the human heart
in conflict with itself.*
WILLIAM FAULKNER

# CHAPTER

# 1

The night that Ed and I decided to leave Atlanta, we were nearing the end of our evening walk when a fire engine tore by with lights flashing and siren howling. If we had been inside our house, the whole foundation would have shaken, as it did every time a dump truck or city bus passed by. Outside the house, the tremor took place in our bodies, as we shied from the weight of the metal hurtling by. We were both used to this. Both of us had lived in Atlanta for half our lives by then, and up to that point the benefits of living in a big city had outweighed the costs. The human diversity was worth the traffic. The great restaurants were worth the smog. The old friends were worth the burgeoning strip malls; and the old neighborhood was worth the property taxes, even if my car stereo had been stolen twice in one year. I do not know why the balance shifted that particular night, but it did. When the din of the fire engine had receded far enough for me to hear him, Ed looked straight ahead and said, "If we don't leave the city, I'm going to die sooner than I have to."

I knew what he meant. As one of four priests in a big downtown parish, I was engaged in work so meaningful that there was no place to stop. Even on a slow day, I left church close to dark. Sixty-hour weeks were normal, hovering closer to eighty during the holidays. Since my job involved visiting parishioners in hospitals and nursing homes on top of a heavy administrative load, the to-do list was never done. More often, I simply abandoned it when I felt my mind begin to coast like a car out of gas. Walking outside of whatever building I had been in, I was often surprised by how warm the night was, or how cold. I was so immersed in indoor human dramas that I regularly lost track of the seasons. When a fresh breeze lifted the hairs on my neck, I had to stop and think, Does that wind signal the end of spring or the beginning of autumn? What month is this? What year, for that matter?

In the ICU, nurses wrote details like these on blackboards to help their dazed patients hang on to reality. Most days I could name the president of the United States, but my daily contact with creation had shrunk to the distance between my front door and the driveway. The rest of my life took place inside: inside the car, inside the church, inside my own head. On the nights when Ed and I walked, I sometimes talked with my eyes fixed on the moving pavement for more than a mile before an owl's cry or a chorus of cicadas brought me, literally, to my senses.

Only then did I smell the honeysuckle that had been there all along or notice the ghostly blossoms on the magnolia trees that deepened the shadows on more than one front lawn. The effect was immediate, like a shot of adrenaline straight to the heart. All these earthly goods were medicine for what ailed me, evidence that the same God who had breathed the world into being was still breathing. There was so much life springing up all around me that the runoff alone was enough to revive me. When it did, I could not imagine why I had stayed away so long. Why did I seal myself off from all this freshness? On what grounds did I fast from the daily bread of birdsong and starlight?

The obvious answer was that I was a priest, with more crucial things to do than to go for a walk around the park. I had been blessed with work so purposeful that taking time off from it felt like a betrayal of divine trust. I was a minister of the gospel in a congregation of close to two thousand people, set in the center of a city of never-ending human need. When I went home at night, I drove past homeless people pushing rusted grocery carts down empty streets, and hospitals with all their windows lit. I carried with me all the stories I had heard that day, from the young woman who had just discovered that the baby she carried inside of her was deformed to the old man who had just lost his wife of fifty-seven years. I knew that I would hear more such stories the next day, and the day after that, with no healing power but the power of listening at my command.

I knew that there were wonderful stories out there too, but most people do not need a priest to listen to those stories. Plus, when you are tired, you cannot hear those stories anyway. You get jumpy, like a fireman who has just finished a double shift and cannot go out to eat without expecting to hear a big explosion from the kitchen. After a bad couple of nights on call, even the candles on the table can make you nervous. In my case, I knew I was tired when I started seeing things that were not there. Driving home in the evening, I would see the crushed body of a brown dog lying in the middle of the street up ahead, causing a great howl of grief to rise up inside of me. By the time I reached the corpse, it had turned into a crushed cardboard box instead. When this happened twice in a row, I knew I was tired.

I had remedies in place to help me keep my pace. I climbed the StairMaster at the gym. I paid monthly visits to a pastoral counselor. I planned vacations to exotic places where there were no telephones. Some guilt was involved in all but the first of these, since I had the idea that the practice of ministry alone should nourish me. Maybe I had read *The Diary of a Country Priest* too often, or maybe I was too much of a romantic, but I thought that God would keep depositing funds in my account whenever my balance got low. I thought that all I had to do was give myself fully to the work, and God would keep me in business. Instead, I was seeing a lot of corpses in the road, and telling myself they were not really there did nothing to diminish my grief.

On the night of the fire engine, when Ed saw where his life was leading him if he did not take a detour soon, I piggybacked on his prophecy. Maybe we could move someplace with fewer sirens and more trees, I thought. Maybe I could serve a smaller church with less complicated needs.

The next weekend we began taking day trips out of the city to see if we could imagine living anywhere else. The idea was to skip right over the suburbs and head for the countryside, but our requirements were such that our options were few. We needed some place with a vacant Episcopal church in it or at least an area where I could start one. We needed a town where Ed could move his engineering business and find some good people to work with him. We needed a sizable piece of land that suited us both, preferably with an old farmhouse on it. We needed to stay within driving distance of family.

We needed a lot.

Since we are both intuitive types, we do not decide things as much as we gravitate toward them. This is not very theological language, I know, but on the subject of divine guidance I side with Susan B. Anthony. "I distrust those people who know so well what God wants them to do," she once said, "because I notice it always coincides with their own desires." Having been somewhat of an expert on the sanctification of my own desires, I try not to pin them on God anymore. At the same time, I recognize the enormous energy in them, which strikes me as something that God might be able to use.

When I read the stories in the Bible about people such as Sarah, Jacob, or David, what stands out is not their virtue but their very strong wants. Sarah wanted her son to prevail over Hagar's son, Jacob wanted his older brother's blessing, and David wanted Bathsheba. While these cravings clearly bought them all kinds of well-deserved trouble, they also kept these characters very, very alive. Their desires propelled them in ways that God could use, better than God could use those who never colored outside the lines. Based on their example, I decided to take responsibility for what I wanted and to trust God to take it from there.

Intuition may be one way of speaking about how God does that—takes things from here to there, I mean. Since intuition operates lower down than the frontal lobe, it is not easy to talk about how it works. In general, I tend not to pay much attention to it until I have completed all of my research, compiled my lists of pros and cons, and made a rational decision based on facts. Then, when I cannot sleep because the rational decision seems all wrong to me, I start paying attention to the gyroscope of my intuition, which operates below the radar of my reason. I pay attention to recurring dreams and interesting coincidences. I let my feelings off the leash and follow them around. When something moves in my peripheral vision, I leave the path to investigate, since it would be a shame to walk right by a burning bush. At this point, reason is all but useless to me. All that remains is trust. Will I trust my intuition or won't I? The more I do, the more intuitive I become. This is as close as I can come to describing the guidance of the Holy Spirit.

After weeks of driving around, Ed and I both felt strong pulls to the mountains of northeast Georgia. Part of it was the sheer beauty of the place, with cows grazing green pastures in front of blue mountains. A mechanical engineer with a farmer's heart, Ed had come into our marriage with two tractors that he was aching to use. I was looking for a smaller church and a different vocabulary. After ten years of focusing on the needs of an urban congregation, I wondered how the gospel might sound in a different landscape. I knew how to speak to people who worked in skyscrapers and volunteered in homeless shelters, but what did I have to say to people who lived on dirt roads and kept bees?

One weekend we set out for Clarkesville, population 1500, tucked up in the corner of Georgia between North and South Carolina. An old resort town, Clarkesville had an equally old Episcopal church with a full-time and much-beloved rector in place. This meant that the church was not available, but since our goal was to see what life outside Atlanta was like, we went anyway. About ninety minutes out of the city, we headed north on highway 197, past an old gristmill with a working water wheel and pastures full of spotted cows. When we stopped for gas about a mile out of town I bought a copy of the *Northeast Georgian,* which turned out to be the local weekly. I had heard about weekly newspapers, but I had never actually read one. Who could wait a whole week for the news? What kind of community generated so few notable events that every seven days was often enough to catch up on them?

While the headlines were forgettable, things became more interesting with the arrest report on page two. Almost two dozen people had gotten in trouble the previous week, with crimes that ranged from public drunkenness to failure to pay child support. Their full names were printed along with their ages and offenses, which struck me as a print version of putting them in stocks in front of the courthouse. What would it be like to open the newspaper and see your name there? *Barbara Brown Taylor, 40, driving with expired license, no proof of insurance.* "Do we have proof of insurance with us?" I asked Ed.

Page six featured photographs of Rotary members handing giant replicas of bank checks to high school students, along with backyard gardeners holding huge yellow squash. The fiftieth wedding anniversary announcements were on the

same page as the birth announcements. There were almost as
many letters to the editor as there were specials at the grocery
store, and the obituaries included someone who died in her
bed when her house trailer caught fire during the night.

While we waited for the first of Clarkesville's two stoplights
to change, I read the letter board at the Magic Spray Car
Wash. "God Loves You" it said. "Doesn't That Car Need A
Bath?" The same block held a Huddle House and a Hardee's
separated by a used car lot. Things improved closer to town,
where a couple of antebellum mansions served as bed-and-
breakfast inns. Just past the second one stood an old church
that was the same vintage as the one we were looking for, but
the sign outside said First Presbyterian Church. We kept
going, past two banks, two funeral homes, and a small string of
shops that led to the town square.

Since Grace Episcopal Church had been in Clarkesville for a
hundred and fifty years, I figured that it would be easy to find,
but I was wrong. The man at the filling station said that he had
never heard of it, and there were no trademark blue "The Episcopal Church Welcomes You" signs pointing the way. If I had
been able to recognize it, this was my first indication that Episcopalians were an introduced species in rural north Georgia.
While kudzu had not been around for half as long, it was better
accepted than a church with a name that was as hard to say as it
was to spell. "Espicopal" (rhymes with "despicable") was the
local variation that I would hear most often in years to come,
but on that first day all I wanted was to lay eyes on the place.

With the help of a Habersham County map, I finally found
Green Street. Ed drove as I counted off the three blocks from

Washington Street. At the corner of Green and Wilson, I looked up to see a white frame chapel with huge clear glass windows and green shutters sitting in an old grove of white pines. The only indication that we had found the right place was a historical marker out front. Grace Episcopal Church, it told us, was organized December 12, 1838, for three local families and "many coastal families" who summered in Clarkesville. The square acre of land was purchased for $100 in 1839. When Bishop Stephen Elliott Jr. consecrated the new church in 1842, he declared it a "very neat wooden building, with tower and bell, prettily located, and an ornament to the village."

I had not seen anything so clean and upright since my last trip to New England. The small porch of the church was supported by four square columns. Just to the left of the double front doors, a thick rope leading to the bell tower was draped over a hook just taller than a second grader. The churchyard bore evidence of having been loved by generations of gardeners. Native azaleas and mountain laurel grew among stones that someone had placed in pleasing constellations, long enough ago for moss to grow on them. Ancient boxwoods grew under the six sash windows, and there was a large holly out front.

Simply to stand in the presence of that building was to rest. Peace poured off the white boards and caught me in its wake as the sighing of the pines reminded me to breathe. When I did, I could feel the clenched muscle of my mind relax. My shoulders came down from around my ears. I shook out my arms and put my hands flat on the side of the church. Was this what happened to wood that had soaked up a hundred and fifty years' worth of prayers? Did all of that devotion seep into the grain like incense so that any passerby could catch a whiff of it?

When I walked up the painted gray steps to the porch, the old boards creaked under my feet. I stood in front of the heavy doors, which had survived so many humid summers that they scarcely met anymore. When I bent over to look through the huge keyhole, I could see a narrow slice of the sanctuary but no more. I tried the doorknob, mostly to feel the cool metal under my hand, but when it turned I was not really surprised. The generosity of this church was already established fact in my mind.

I stepped into the smell of candle wax, old books, and sun on wood. To either side of me, identical red-carpeted stairways led up to a tiny balcony, which was supported by four pillars in front of me. Besides the red under my feet, the only three colors inside the church were the white of the walls, the brown of the woodwork, and the shiny brass of the processional cross that was attached to the front of the high Victorian pulpit.

There was no central aisle for weddings nor space up front for baptisms. When the church was built, such socially significant occasions would have occurred back home in Charleston or Savannah. Instead, three sections of boxed pews filled the small space between the front door and the altar rail. Opening and shutting the little gates, I counted the seats. There were five in each pew on the left, four in the middle, and five on the right. In a pinch, the place could seat eighty-five people.

The church I served in downtown Atlanta seated four hundred and fifty people, not once but twice on Sunday mornings, with an earlier service in the chapel at 8:00 AM. Grace Church was a dollhouse by comparison, which was a large part of its charm. This was a church I could get my arms around, a church in which I could see every face and know every name. As the sunlight pouring through the windows raised a toasty smell from the old pews, I imagined sitting on people's porches drinking iced glasses of sweet tea while they told me about their lives. I imagined celebrating communion with them while the wind pushed clouds across the sky and made waves of light lap over the room I was standing in. Of course this church was not available. I needed to remember that this church had a longtime rector who was not going anywhere.

Like every preacher who had walked in before me, I could not resist taking in the view from the high pulpit. In a space so small, it was a true antique, left over from a time when preachers really did speak from on high to sinners down below. Climbing the small staircase, I found the aerie stacked with old glass vases, a few green cubes of Styrofoam, and a broken chair. Clearly, I was the first preacher who had been up there in a while. This told me two important things: (1) In this church, clergy engaged the congregation at eye level, and (2) the altar guild was out of storage space.

Shifting the broken chair to make room for my feet, I straightened up to see the pipe organ in the balcony for the first time. The gold-painted pipes reached all the way to the ceiling without an inch to spare. They were housed in a carved wooden cabinet that looked as old as the church. Looking straight into the balcony, I realized that the slaves who had once sat there had occupied the best seats in the house. From the high pulpit, the same preacher who looked down on their owners could have met the servants' eyes straight on.

Climbing back down the stairs, I let myself out the altar gate and sat down on the red velvet kneeler. There were so many panes of wavy glass in the windows that the place swam with dust motes dazzled by the light. The branches of a hemlock swayed in the breeze outside. When Ed touched me on the shoulder, I looked up at him and said, "I want this church."

B y falling in love with a building before I ever met the people who worshiped in it, I participated in a popular misunderstanding of the word *church*. Properly speaking, the noun refers not to a piece of real estate but to a community of people, who may or may not meet inside of a church building. As I learned in the weeks following my first visit, Grace Church met for the first time in the living room of the Reverend Ezra Kellogg, a missionary from New York, in 1838. The congregation of some thirty souls that formed that day met wherever they could for the next several years, and it was not until four years later that the church took up permanent residence in a building at the corner of Green and Wilson Streets.

The village of Clarkesville had been on the map for only about twenty years at that point, carved out of Indian Territory by a treaty with the Cherokee Nation that was rendered moot when President Jackson signed the Removal Act of 1830. As defeated Cherokee and Creek people were herded down the Trail of Tears toward Oklahoma, wealthy planters from

Charleston and Savannah arrived to take their land. Fleeing the heat and danger of fever back home, these aristocrats settled in the breezy foothills of the Appalachians. Resort hotels and boardinghouses sprang up around the Clarkesville square as more well-to-do families built elaborate summer homes in the surrounding countryside.

Once their own congregation was up and running, the people of Grace Church established several missions in the area. They built a chapel of ease called Holy Cross three miles out of town near the minister's home so that he could hold services there when the roads were impassable by horse and buggy. In 1848 they commissioned a five-rank tracker organ from the Erben Organ Factory in New York, and in 1852 a church bell cast by George Hildbrook of East Medway, Massachusetts, arrived by wagon for installation in the bell tower.

In 1861 the Civil War put a lid on all such expansiveness. When the South was defeated four years later, Grace Church's heyday was over. Newly destitute, the founding families of the "snap bean church" (so named because the congregation stayed in town only until the last crop of summer beans was harvested) either gave up their summer homes around Clarkesville or sold their property on the coast in order to settle in the mountains full-time. By the Second World War, church membership had declined to the point that regular services were suspended. If nearby Calvary Church had not helped with the bills, the roof of Grace Church would have caved in. The two congregations merged in the 1970s, choosing the Clarkesville church building for their home, and by the 1980s newly named Grace-Calvary Church was once again healthy enough to establish missions in the area.

As anyone who studies congregations knows, history matters. The story of a church's birth tends to shape that community's identity for the rest of its life, with each new generation adding its own variations to the foundational themes. In my case, Clarkesville's history as a summer resort town meant that newcomers like me were welcomed more warmly than we might have been elsewhere. The "been heres" were used to the "come heres" and had even learned how to make some money off them.

On our first visit to Clarkesville, Ed and I got used to answering the question "Where ya'll from?" We heard it at the Yogurt Shoppe on the square, at Duncan Oil's full-service filling station on highway 105, and at the Mark of the Potter on highway 197, where tourists from all over the Southeast came to buy hand-thrown coffee mugs and pitch fish food at the obese trout lolling in the Soque River out back. Even though we heard a rumor that no local auto mechanic would either tow or work on my old Saab, everyone we ran into was friendly enough.

At the church level, Grace-Calvary's history meant that local families and summer residents had shared lay leadership for more than a century. While certain names showed up over and over again in the parish register, there was no local cabal intent on preserving its power in church affairs. The work, the power, and the food at the parish picnics were all pretty well distributed so that the line between newcomers and old-timers was often hard to find.

If anything, Grace-Calvary was distinguished by how little time most clergy stayed there. Between 1838 and 1990, the church had twenty-one rectors, only four of whom lasted more than ten years. Like most congregants, the people of Grace-Calvary were sorry to see some of these ministers go even as they helped others leave. Every now and then, they simply resolved to wait a minister out. After the Reverend William Walton arrived in 1895, he decided to replace the high pulpit with a dorsal curtain on a pole. Vestryman William Kollock carefully numbered each piece of the beloved pulpit as it came down, stored the parts in his barn, and happily put it back up again fourteen years later when Mr. Walton finally left.

After that, the average tenure for clergy was a little less than five years, with some of them leaving more dramatically than others. When I first visited, the congregation was under the care of Saint Julian Mustard Lachicotte, a legendary character whom I knew from clergy conferences as a bourbon connoisseur with a wicked sense of humor. Not only was "Saint" part of his legal, baptized name, but Julian was also the youngest of eight children from a prominent South Carolina family. A divorced chain-smoker with a bald head, dark arched eyebrows, and a house full of antiques, he was known affectionately by some around town as "Louie Quatorze."

Under his nine years of leadership, Grace-Calvary grew and stabilized. The church paid off its debts, established an endowment fund, and organized a new mission in nearby Blairsville. Julian also worked with clergy from other denominations to start several local ministries, including Habitat for Humanity and Circle of Hope, a battered women's shelter. When he did not show up for work on the Tuesday after All Saints' Day in November 1990, two members of the church went to his house to find Julian dead on his kitchen floor. At his funeral, the old sash windows of the church had to be propped open so that the overflow crowd standing in the churchyard could hear the bishop commend Saint Julian's soul to God.

When I heard the news back in Atlanta, I was stunned, not only because Julian was such a good man, but also because I had just coveted his church. I waited three days before I called the bishop and asked him to put my name on the list of candidates to fill the new vacancy at Grace-Calvary Church.

# CHAPTER

## 3

Almost a decade earlier, a shirt box had arrived at my house the week before I was ordained a deacon in the Episcopal Church. The customs form, filled out by a shipping clerk at J. Wippell and Company, Ltd., in Exeter, England, said "clergy apparel." Inside the box were three black, long-sleeved shirts, three stiff white plastic clerical collars, and three pairs of brass-plated collar studs. As long as I had waited for them, my stomach lurched at the sight of these new clothes. Who did I think I was? More to the point, who would other people think I was once I put these things on?

Since I had been a late-blooming flower child, my choice of vocation struck many who knew me as odd. When I announced that I was going to seminary straight out of college, my mother turned from doing the dishes at the kitchen sink and said, "You *will* get over this." Even my college adviser worried about me. Although I had majored in religion, my transcript listed more courses in mysticism and environmental ethics than it did in Bible and theology. I had no intention of being ordained, which was a good thing since I did not belong to any church that might ordain me. I was simply drawn to spend as much time reading, thinking, and writing about God as I could, and seminary seemed to offer me the best chance of doing that.

As hard as I have tried to remember the exact moment when I fell in love with God, I cannot do it. My earliest memories are bathed in a kind of golden light that seemed to embrace me as surely as my mother's arms. The Divine Presence was strongest outdoors, and most palpable when I was alone. When I think of my first cathedral, I am back in a field behind my parents' house in Kansas, with every stalk of prairie grass lit up from within. I can hear the entire community of crows, grasshoppers, and tree frogs who belong to this field with me. The smell of the grass is so sweet that it perfumes me from within, while the sun heating the top of my head brings out my own fragrance too. There is more in this field than I will ever be able to discover—not only the abandoned shells of land snails and the shed feathers of blue jays but also round holes in the earth that might have been dug by field mice or black snakes, but I will never know which, because as long as I lie there watching the hole, no creature ever appears to go in or come out of it.

This does not really matter because lying there is very good. My skin is happy on the black dirt, which speaks a language my bones understand. If I roll over and think only about the places on my back that are touching the ground, then pretty soon I cannot tell whether I am pressing down on the earth or the earth is pressing up on me. The feeling is the same as when my father holds me up in the swimming pool, teaching me to float. As frightened as I am of getting water up my nose, I gradually relax into his open arms, trusting him to bear me up. One day he will let go of me, but he has not yet done so. Until he does, there is no better feeling in the world than resting on his open arms with my body half in and half out of the pool, the sun on my face, and enough water in my ears so that all I can really hear is the beating of my heart.

I am floating in this field, held up toward the sun by the black dirt under my back. I am this earth's child, and I know it. When I am done lying here, I will visit the small crystal stream that runs through this field to see what is moving in it today. The Presence will be there too, lighting up everything that moves. I have met salamanders there, tadpoles, crayfish, and water bugs. I have watched the moss on the bottom ripple as the water runs over it. Years later, I will discover that this was no crystal stream but a drainage ditch. The difference between these two descriptions of the same place will screw with my sense of reality for a long time. Is the Divine Presence in the world, or in my eye?

Because I was not brought up in church, I had no religious language for what happened in that golden-lit field or in any of the other woods or fields that followed it. I had no picture in my mind of a fantastic-looking old man named God who lived in a heaven above my head. I did not know to close my eyes and bow my head to speak to this God, and I certainly did not know that there was anything wrong with that field or what I experienced in it. If anyone had tried to tell me that creation was fallen or that I should care more for heaven than earth, I would have gone off to lie in the sweet grass by myself.

When I was seven I went to church for the first time, where I got the same feeling of being held that I knew from the field. I furthermore got the impression that the people who were there that morning had figured out a way of talking about that feeling. They seemed to know where it came from, who was responsible for it, what it meant, and how to respond to it. They read from a big book that apparently taught them these things, and when the minister talked he seemed to know more than anyone about how special the feeling was and how important it was to thank God for it. I was impressed, with him and with the singing, if not with the readings from the book. An hour later, I was back in the car with my family, permanently hooked on finding out more about God.

Because we moved a lot, and because my parents were not as taken with divinity as I was, my religious quest was largely do-it-yourself. I paid careful attention to movies with Christians in them, which spanned the gamut from *Spartacus* to *The Lilies of the Field.* I read everything Pearl Buck ever wrote with a missionary in it. While I read Rumer Godden's *In This House of Brede,* I longed for a mother superior, and when *The Flying Nun* appeared on television, I found the nun far less interesting than her hat. I hitched rides with friends to the churches and synagogues they attended without ever finding what I was looking for. The services lasted for only an hour, for one thing, and I never got to ask any questions during them, for another. When I went to Sunday school, it was like being back in regular school again except that the subject matter was different. The teachers worked from a set curriculum with specific things in it that they wanted me to learn, but I was hard-pressed to find any connection between those things and the Divine Presence that I knew from the field.

By then my family had moved far from Kansas, but the Presence was still with me. On warm Georgia nights I would climb over the fence of the golf club near my house and walk the manicured greens bathed in moonlight. There was a crystal stream there too, which ran under a small wooden footbridge between two fairways. Some nights I would sit there until the stars came out, seeing them first in the water and then seeing them in the sky. During the summer months, when the fireflies were out, it was hard to know whether the lights belonged to heaven or to earth. This is a line that has remained forever blurry for me.

Though it was night instead of day, I still felt held in arms that I could not see. No words came with the feeling. I received no visions or directions, which would have surprised me in any case since the Presence was not outside me. I lived inside the Presence, which placed me in communion with everything around me, including my parents and my two sisters in the house I had left behind, every neighbor behind the lit windows that stretched down my street, and all the creatures I could hear rustling in the dark.

Day by day, the practical implication of this feeling of communion was that I could not walk by a hurt thing without hurting too. When I learned that the white rats in my father's psychology lab were going to be gassed, I begged him to bring them home to me. When I learned that the mice at the pet store were being sold for snake food, I spent my entire allowance on them. After they gnawed through the wooden toy box that I kept them in, a whole tribe of brown and white spotted mice sprang up in our basement, but my parents knew better than to stanch my bleeding heart. They let me bring home hurt birds, orphaned opossums, and at least one hungry dog, even though my success rate was less than 1 percent with everything but the dog.

The number of graves in the backyard never deterred me from picking up the next orphan or cripple. Caring for creatures who could not care for themselves offered me a larger sense of purpose than playing Monopoly or collecting stamps. I was much happier with a hurt bird than I was with most people, not least because the bird seemed happier to see me. Sitting quietly together, we both got better. We understood each other, and, in the inexplicable alchemy of compassion, my care for the bird gave real comfort to me.

If you talk to most clergy long enough, you can usually pinpoint the moment when they first received a call to ministry. Nine times out of ten, it did not come straight from God. Instead, it came from a grandmother, a father, a sick sibling, a wounded bird. Sometimes the call came with spoken words, such as, "You're good at this," or "I need your help badly." Other times the words arose inside, such as, "This needs fixing and I think I know how."

The effort to untangle the human words from the divine seems not only futile to me but also unnecessary, since God works with what is. God uses whatever is usable in a life, both to speak and to act, and those who insist on fireworks in the sky may miss the electricity that sparks the human heart. In my case, priesthood was as natural to me as breathing, as simple as picking up a hurt thing and taking it home either to heal or to bury.

My compassion did not extend quite as naturally to human beings, since I had ample evidence that they were as likely to cause hurt as to suffer it themselves. As a preternaturally tall and bookish child, I was used to being sat on during recess by my classmates, who would groan out loud when the teacher forced me to play on their teams. They groaned for good reason, since I could not throw a ball or swing a bat without suffering the torments of hell. When I made up for this physical disability by excelling in class, my popularity rating went into single digits and stayed there for most of my public school career. Even the people I thought of as my friends looked embarrassed when I asked them to sign my yearbook.

My religious experiments continued through high school and into college, gaining urgency with the escalation of the war in Vietnam. By the time I was eighteen, I had witnessed the assassinations of two Kennedys and one King. Boys my age were being sent to Southeast Asia to fight a dreadful war that few of us understood. When some of us stopped attending our college classes to protest this war, the professors who joined us in the quadrangle were the ones from the religion department. Under their tutelage, I added *nonviolent resistance* and *social justice* to my vocabulary. I discovered the God of the Hebrew prophets. I read Dietrich Bonhoeffer and Paul Tillich, who spoke of the Divine Presence in language that far surpassed any of the language I had heard in churches.

So of course when it came time to decide what to do with my life, I decided to go to seminary. What else do you do when

you are in love with God? Even if ordination is the farthest
thing from your mind, even if you cannot find a church big
enough to hold all that you know to be true about God, what
do you do with this strange attraction but go where other
people go when they feel it too? If I had been born in another
time and place, I might have headed to a convent or to a small
beehive-shaped hut made of stone on a holy island. I might
even have found a shaman to lead me deeper into the mysteries. In my own time and place, I was not aware of so many options. When I put my strong sense of the Divine Presence
together with my irresistible urge to help hurt things, seminary
kept coming up as the next stop on my map. If I was drawn to
God, then surely that meant I was drawn to religion, and if I
was drawn to religion, then surely that meant I should go to
seminary. When the Rockefeller Foundation offered me a free
trial year at the school of my choice, I took it as an omen.

I sent my application to Yale Divinity School, Yale Divinity
School accepted it, and in the early fall of 1973 I pulled out of
my parents' driveway with my green Saab 99 packed to the roof.
I had never lived more than a mile from home. I had never
driven farther than South Carolina by myself. When I looked
in the rearview mirror at the bottom of the driveway, I saw my
dog sitting there with one ear up and one down, wagging his tail
against the asphalt as I drove away. I cried most of the way to
Virginia, dried up in Maryland, and became euphoric in New
York. By the time I arrived in New Haven I was so elated by
the stone gargoyles on all the buildings that I parked my car in
front of a phone booth on College Street, stopping traffic while
I called my mother to tell her that I had arrived in Oz.

I went to seminary the same way some people sail around the world. On no particular timetable, I let the wind carry me. Under the care of no bishop, I took any course that interested me. I became friends with Lebanese Presbyterians, Minnesota Lutherans, and Franciscan monks. I read brain-busting books, learned ancient languages, prayed tortuous prayers. When I discovered Christ Episcopal Church my second year, a whole new sea opened up to me. I read the poetry of George Herbert and John Donne, along with everything Charles Williams ever wrote. I learned my way around the 1928 Book of Common Prayer, attending High Mass until I could sing the Nicene Creed in my sleep.

For the first time in my life, I had found a church where the Divine Presence felt as strong to me inside as it did outside. When I entered that sacred cave, I not only lost track of time, I also lost track of my self. From the moment the thurifer passed down the central aisle, swinging the censer in a cloud of sweet smoke, to the moment the organist lifted his fingers from the last chord, I became part of a body far larger than my self. As this body stood to sing, kneeled to pray, and stood again to declare its faith, I did my part without feeling apart. The feeling of communion was already so intense that I did not go forward for the bread and wine. I let the body go forward for me, while I sat there sensing God's pleasure. Before Christ Church, I thought that worship was something people cooked up by themselves. At Christ Church, I discovered worship that took place inside God's own heart. The divine pleasure was the pleasure of a mother with her baby at her breast.

After a couple of months of this, I made an appointment with the rector to announce that I wanted to become an Episcopalian. Pursing his lips, he laced his fingers together and sat back in his desk chair. "Dearie, why don't you tell me your story?" he said, so I did. I told him about my baptism in the Catholic Church when I was six weeks old and my trip to the Methodist Church when I was seven. I told him about Jack, my redheaded Baptist boyfriend, who persuaded me to be baptized again by immersion when I was sixteen, but how that did not last very long after Jack and I broke up.

I told him about how during my sophomore year at college I accepted Jesus into my heart under some pressure from the Navigators and became something of a Jesus freak before discovering the Sunday night suppers at the Newman House, where I learned about Thomas Merton and Dorothy Day from Father Joe Genessee. I told him how I had joined Central Presbyterian Church in Atlanta after my first semester at seminary because I felt self-conscious about having no church affiliation and because Central had such a strong ministry of social justice in the city.

Now that I had found the Episcopal Church, I told him, I could see how I had moved from one congregation to another based on vagaries of location and personality, including my own. In the Episcopal Church, I had finally discovered something more lasting than that. I had discovered a history, a theology, and a liturgy that spoke to me, offering me words for all that I had not been able to say to God. Please, I said, I wanted to be confirmed in the Episcopal Church.

When I was through, this good priest unlaced his fingers

and smiled at me. "Dearie," he said, reaching over so that his chair squeaked as he patted the back of my hand, "you are an ecclesiastical harlot. Let's be sure you're really in love this time, hmm?" For the next year, he directed both my reading and my prayers. He cooked roast duck for me, found things for me to do around church, and suffered my adoration of him. At the end of this process, he agreed to present me to the bishop. I was confirmed in the Episcopal Church when I was twenty-five years old, just weeks before my graduation from seminary.

In this way, I found the church that is still my home, though I still had no intention of being ordained. In the first place, I could not imagine myself in brocade vestments, taking a leading role in the divine drama that I witnessed every Sunday. At what point did a person decide that he or she was holy enough to do something like that? Being a priest seemed only slightly less dicey to me than being chief engineer at a nuclear plant. In both cases, one needed to know how to approach great power without loosing great danger and getting fried in the process. All in all, I was happier in the pew.

Yet even there I had some reservations about the whole setup. If the purpose of the church were to equip all God's people for ministry to the world—as I was learning in seminary—then what sense did it make to designate one of those people "the minister" in a congregation? The minute you set someone apart like that, didn't you give everyone else license to say, "Don't look at me—*she's* the minister"?

In the same way, if the minister's job were to support church members as they engaged their vocations in the world, then what sense did it make to locate that person inside the four safe walls of a church? A mobile unit would have made more sense, like one of those libraries on wheels that goes wherever people need books. As strongly as I was being drawn to worship at Christ Church, my heart remained in the world. I belonged among the laity, not the clergy.

After graduation, I discovered that a divinity degree was not a big door opener, at least not for someone who did not intend to be ordained. I applied for a job teaching religion at a private school in Atlanta; but when the principal asked me what sports I could coach, I knew that I had better keep looking. I worked as a cocktail waitress and a camp counselor before landing a full-time secretarial job at a United Methodist seminary. While this meant I worked with wonderful people, the pay was so low that I sometimes stole rolls of toilet paper from the women's restroom to save expenses at home.

Around the same time, I began attending a large downtown church. Having searched in vain for Christ Church South, I settled for an incenseless, folksy liturgy in a congregation committed to urban ministry. At Saint Luke's, the holy danger I had once experienced at the altar was transferred to the parish hall, where hundreds of homeless men and women showed up for soup and sandwiches each week. On Sundays most of them were gone, due largely to the policeman who directed traffic in the parking lot, but their smell lingered in the parish hall under a thin haze of Lysol. Although I never lost the sense of belonging to a church with two separate congregations, Saint Luke's taught me to see the Divine Presence in human faces, and especially in those that least resembled mine.

The ordination of women to the priesthood had been legal

for only about a year at that time, so the clergy were all men. The rector was committed to a woman's presence at the altar, however, and had hired a female seminarian as a part-time parish assistant. When she was ordained and moved on, he asked me to take her place. "Strange travel suggestions are dancing lessons from God," Kurt Vonnegut wrote in one of his novels, which is how my vocation has unfolded all of my life.

In this way, I became the seminarian at Saint Luke's Episcopal Church, showing up every Sunday morning to compete with the other lay ministers for borrowed vestments that had not been sweated on too much. My outfit was a plain white cassock alb with a white cotton cincture. The clergy, who owned their robes, added colorful stoles that identified them as priests or deacons. As they talked to one another, they slid the ends of their stoles through elaborate loops in the cinctures around their waists, which entailed some impressive rope work. Most of them could do it without even looking, like origami masters folding paper cranes in the dark. Since my cincture required no more than a single knot, I had plenty of time to tug at the hems and brush off the shoulders of those whose outfits were more complicated than mine. Then we reviewed our roles, stood in a small circle to pray, and lined up in reverse order, with the lay ministers at the head of the procession and the priest who would preside over communion at the end.

After all the hubbub of preparation and the press of people at the door of the church, there was nothing quite like taking that first step down the aisle as the opening hymn began. The crucifer heaved the brass processional cross heavenward. Watching it made the rest of us lift our heads, as we began our slow march toward the altar through a sea of sound. No one could touch us anymore. The ancient drama had begun. All around us, hundreds of otherwise fractious people sang in unison. The organ covered all our flaws. For once in our lives, we were doing one thing instead of many things, and we were doing it surprisingly well.

At the communion rail, people knelt to let themselves be fed. First the priest bent toward them with the bread, then I bent toward them with the wine. They reached for the chalice as I moved it toward their lips. When our hands met on the silver cup, there was a charged moment in which we became one body, less in theory than in fact. While I remained aware that it was Bill or Ann or a perfect stranger before me, I could not summon up any of the feelings that might have accompanied that identification in the fellowship hall or the grocery store. The recognition took place at a deeper lever, where one fully exposed human being rested for a moment in the presence of another.

Artifice did not stand a chance in that atmosphere, which was why I focused on people's hands instead of their faces. An unguarded face is a deep well; you don't go there casually, without ropes or lamps. So I practiced what some religious orders still call "custody of the eyes," not only because eyes are portholes, but also because one does not gaze directly upon the Holy and live. After it was all over, the lay assistants gathered around the altar to help the clergy finish up the leftover bread and wine. Then we handed the empty vessels back to the celebrant and prepared to leave the church in the same order that we had arrived.

Back in the vesting room, we all talked and jostled as we changed our clothes. I loosened the cincture around my waist, popped the snaps on my white robe, and put it back in the closet with the others. The clergy did the same thing, with one significant difference. Even after they removed their Sunday vestments, they were still in uniform. The rest of the team could walk out of the church without anyone guessing what we did for a living, but the clergy walked out with white clerical collars, which announced their identities to every passerby.

Before I had been at Saint Luke's a year, I began wanting to wear one too. When I served communion, visited the sick, taught the youth, and sat with the elderly, I felt lit up inside. Tending the Divine Presence in others, I became more aware of it in myself. I also felt useful to God. While this did nothing to resolve my theoretical problems with ordination, I was so drawn to the work of ministry that I knew I wanted to keep on doing it. I furthermore wanted to do it full-time, and in my mind there was only one way to do that. While I could not use the word *priest* in a sentence that began with *I,* that was what I wanted to be.

In the language of the Church, I was sensing a call. In the Episcopal Church, however, that was far from enough. God does not ordain people directly, as more than one bishop would tell me in years to come. The Church ordains people in whom it recognizes clear gifts for ministry, and the process of discerning those gifts takes as long as it takes. In my case, it took close to five years to go through the screening program, meet the additional requirements, make my way through the committees, and pass the exams. I also quit the process at least twice, but in the end I was given permission to order my new clothes.

Never having worn a collar myself, I could not imagine how it felt from the inside, but I had a pretty good idea how it worked from the outside. Once, when I was lost underground in the Times Square subway maze in Manhattan, I was saved from a full-scale panic attack by the sight of a nun in traditional habit. I did not for one moment consider that she was there for any purpose other than to rescue me, and without disabusing me of that notion she kindly pointed me in the right direction.

Picking up the plastic collar in the transatlantic shirt box with my name on it, I remembered her. The collar was not a wimple and I was no nun, but I knew that wearing it would change me because it would change how people responded to me. But first I had to learn how to put it on. After fumbling with the collar, a pair of collar studs, and a black shirt for close to thirty minutes, I finally figured out how they all went together. As I stood in front of the bathroom mirror studying the full effect, a visual memory earlier than the subway nun surfaced in my sight. When I was a little girl riding in the backseat of the family station wagon to visit my relatives in south Georgia, I remember looking out the window to see men in black-and-white pajamas working in the fields.

"Why are those men dressed like that?" I asked my mother. Turning around in her seat, she explained that they were state prisoners, who were dressed like that because the uniforms made them easy to see. If they tried to escape, she said, then the guards could find them quicker, and if they showed up at some farmhouse looking for food, then the people who lived there would know to call the police.

"See how they stand out?" she asked me. Staring out the rear window of the car, I watched them until we were a quarter mile down the road. Then my stomach fluttered as the station wagon crested a small rise and went down the other side. With the convicts gone, I turned around to face the front seat with a bad crick in my neck.

Looking in the bathroom mirror twenty-five years later, I could see how I was going to stand out too. For good or ill, I too would have a hard time escaping. As my beloved rector had told me in seminary, being ordained is not about serving God perfectly but about serving God visibly, allowing other people to learn whatever they can from watching you rise and fall. "You probably won't be much worse than other people," he said, "and you certainly won't be any better, but you will have to let people look at you. You will have to let them see you as you are."

Clearly, the uniform was designed to facilitate that. My new clothes said, "Keep an eye on this person," without granting me any real control over what others made of what they saw. As if to prove my point, my husband of five months walked by the door and stopped to stare at me. I looked at him and tried to smile. He looked at my neck and did not smile.

"Is that really necessary?" Ed asked in a tiny voice, as we both measured the distance the collar put between us. I had been careful to marry him before I married the church, but neither of us had a clue how this blended family was going to work.

L ike all other priests in the Episcopal Church, I was ordained not once but twice. The first ordination, to the diaconate, has biblical roots in the New Testament book called the Acts of the Apostles. When the first apostles became so frazzled by everything they had to do after Jesus was gone, they laid hands on seven good men, setting them in charge of looking after people's physical needs so that the apostles could concentrate on preaching and prayer. In later tradition, these seven became known as deacons, or servants, whose leadership duties included everything from waiting tables to distributing alms among the sometimes scrappy widows of the early Christian community. A few of them, like Stephen and Philip, were also preachers.

The second ordination, to the priesthood, does not show up in the New Testament at all. While the letters of Paul mention deacons, bishops, elders, pastors, teachers, evangelists, and prophets in the early church, there is not a single priest in the whole crowd. In those days, priests were Jewish. Their jobs were tied to the Temple in Jerusalem, where they alone were authorized to perform rituals and conduct services. Because Christianity began as a Jewish movement, however, the language of priesthood carried over. The New Testament letter to the Hebrews calls Jesus a high priest, and by the fourth century the presbyters, or ordained elders, of the church were also called priests. Like their Jewish namesakes, they presided at services where they performed rituals, including the sacrificial feast of Holy Communion with God in Christ.

In the Episcopal Church today, bishops, priests, and deacons are all ordained to embody the gospel, but their job descriptions differ. Bishops oversee the Church, priests tend particular congregations, and deacons help those who cannot help themselves, in what is generally seen as a descending order of ministry. Although there is no question in my mind that bishops really do get to wear the best clothes, those I know well do not regard themselves as having reached any kind of pinnacle.

"Think hard before you do this," one said to me when I told him I wanted to be ordained. "Right now, you have the broadest ministry imaginable. As a layperson, you can serve God no matter what you do for a living, and you can reach out to people who will never set foot inside a church. Once you are ordained, that is going to change. Every layer of responsibility you add is going to narrow your ministry, so think hard before you choose a smaller box."

As surprising as it was, this advice did nothing to dissuade me from wanting to be ordained. The smaller box was, in fact, part of the appeal. After years of working in restaurants, stables, schools, and hospitals, I wanted to work in a church.

After years of visiting the sick in street clothes, I wanted to wear a collar. After years of receiving communion from other hands, I wanted the hands to be mine. While I believed everything I had been taught about the priesthood of all believers, which included the assurance that my ministry in the world was as vital to God's purpose as any ministry in the church, this lay priesthood struck me as something less than full immersion.

I wanted everything I did, all day long, to signal my full commitment to God and God's people. I wanted the uniform, the office, the title, the regular schedule of services, the life of prayer, and the care of souls. I wanted to move in with God on a full-time basis, and ordination looked like my best bet. So I was ordained twice—once as a deacon in Christ's Church and once again as a priest. What I remember best about the first ordination was the opulence of the ceremony. What I remember best about the second was the weight of the hands.

When I was ordained deacon, only the bishop laid his hands on my head. "Therefore, Father," he prayed, pressing down so that I could feel his heavy amethyst ring on my skull, "through Jesus Christ your Son, give your Holy Spirit to Barbara; fill her with grace and power, and make her a deacon in your Church." My head swam with emotion so that I was grateful he had two more deacons to ordain before we all stood up, but everything in this ceremony confirmed the rightness of what I was doing.

When I was ordained priest almost a year later, the bishop invited every other priest who was there to join him in the laying on of hands. I had just promised a whole lot of things during the part of the service called "The Examination." Standing in front of the bishop and the congregation, I had said that I believed I was truly called by God and God's Church to the priesthood. I had promised to respect and be guided by the pastoral direction and leadership of my bishop. I had promised to be diligent in the reading and study of the Holy Scriptures, to endeavor to minister the Word of God and the sacraments of the New Covenant so that the reconciling love of Christ might be known and received, and to be a faithful pastor to all whom I was called to serve. I had promised to do my best to pattern my life and the life of my family in accordance with the teachings of Christ in order to be a wholesome example to my people, and to persevere in prayer, both public and private.

"May the Lord who has given you the will to do these things give you the grace and power to perform them," the bishop said. Then he invited all the other priests to come up to the communion rail. As I knelt before the altar, I heard their vestments rustling behind me while the congregation sang a hymn calling the Holy Spirit to come among us. With my eyes closed and my heart hammering, I felt hands lighting on my head, my shoulders, and my back. At first their weight was comforting, like the weight of a winter quilt. I felt energy pouring into me until my skin went all prickly and my face got hot. Then more hands piled on, and my neck began to hurt. Some of the hands felt wobbly, as if people were leaning in to reach me and were losing their balance in the process. I tried to straighten my back so that I could push back, but it was too late. There was no room left for me to raise myself even a little under that great weight of hands.

The singing had stopped. We had entered the period of silent prayer before the bishop said the prayer of consecration out loud, but I was not feeling prayerful. I was feeling panicky, wondering if I could make it through to the end without standing up and pushing all those hands away from me. Why hadn't anyone warned me that the hands would be so heavy? *Please, please, please,* I prayed, while the entire weight of heaven and earth pressed down on my head. I was getting exactly what I wanted, but I had not realized how much it was going to hurt. Was this God's sly way of letting me know what priesthood was *really* all about? Under the weight of hands, I repented of all my vainglory: of liking the way I looked in a collar, of wanting my own parking space, of needing to be special in hopes of being specially loved. I would serve God, I promised. I would imitate Christ. *Now please let up, just for now, please, let me up.*

While I was repeating the words of this prayer in shorter and shorter bursts, I heard the bishop's voice far above me. "Therefore, Father, through Jesus Christ your Son, give your Holy Spirit to Barbara," he said; "fill her with grace and power, and make her a priest in your church."

When he finished saying that, the weight began to lift. The priests standing around me took back their hands one by one until I could hold my head up again. As they returned to their seats, someone helped me up. I turned and faced the congregation, planting my feet far apart so that I would not fall over. People I loved walked toward me holding my new vestments in their arms. I held still while they tugged a red chasuble over my head and draped a red stole over my shoulders. Then the bishop gave me a Bible, the congregation clapped, and I did what all new priests do at that point in the service. I pronounced the Peace.

"The peace of the Lord be always with you," I said, freshly wise about what that meant.

"And also with you," the people replied. After a very long engagement, it had finally happened. I was a priest in Christ's Church.

Even now, I would prefer a more user-friendly word like *pastor,* but the truth is that an ancient word like *priest* captures the risk of this vocation as well as any word I know. In my lexicon, at least, a priest is someone willing to stand between a God and a people who are longing for one another's love, turning back and forth between them with no hope of tending either as well as each deserves. To be a priest is to serve a God who never stops calling people to do more justice and love more mercy, and simultaneously to serve people who nine times out of ten are just looking for a safe place to rest. To be a priest is to know that things are not as they should be and yet to care for them the way they are. To be a priest is to suspect that there is always something more urgent that you should be doing, no matter what you are doing, and to make peace with the fact that the work will never get done. To be a priest is to wonder sometimes if you are missing the boat altogether, by deferring pleasure in what God has made until you have fixed it up so that it will please God more. "When I wake up in the morning," E. B. White once wrote, "I can't decide whether to enjoy the world or improve the world; that makes it difficult to plan the day."

My early days at All Saints' Church in Atlanta were rich in all that I believed I was called to do. I preached, celebrated the sacraments, visited the sick, and educated the young. I met with the steady stream of people who showed up at the church door looking for food, shelter, medical care, and sympathy. I also proofread the bulletin, recruited Sunday school teachers, kept the roster for nursing home visitations, and attended a great many committee meetings. I did not do any of this alone, of course. I worked as one member of a large team that shared the labor and covered for one another as needed.

Because I was an assistant to the rector and not the rector, I was also free from the extra symbolic weight he carried as *paterfamilias* of the clan. When I finally went home at night, my telephone seldom rang. His number was the one people called when they landed in the emergency room or found a loved one lying lifeless on the bathroom floor. He was also the one people called when they were furious about the way the finance committee was investing the church endowment or the way a Sunday school teacher had spoken to a child or the way the Episcopal Church was treating gay people.

Because he did his job so well, I was able to concentrate on mine, which grew with every day I gave to it for the next nine years. While some clergy justly complain that they are not being allowed to do the things that they were ordained to do, my problem developed more along the lines of choosing among all the things that I *was* ordained to do. With just seven days in a week, where is the time to be a good preacher, teacher, pastor, prophet, celebrant, prayer, writer, foot washer, administrator, community activist, clergy colleague, student of

scripture, and wholesome exemplar of the gospel? When my
friend Matilda lay dying of Lou Gehrig's disease, she said that
she had been prepared all of her life to choose between good
and evil. What no one had prepared her for, she lamented, was
to choose between the good, the better, and the best — and yet
this capacity turned out to be the one she most needed as she
watched the sands of her life run out.

I thought of her often as my time ran out each day. Out of
the long list of things I had promised to be and do at my ordination, the "wholesome example" part was the one that gave me
most pause. I spent a great deal of time trying to be good, but
was good the same as whole? I never lay in the grass anymore,
although I spent one whole week in bed with lower back spasms
that would not quit. I was so busy serving the Divine Presence
that we never got any time alone anymore. On weekends I
wrote sermons, conducted wedding rehearsals, and caught up
on mountains of laundry at home. I knew attorneys and emergency room doctors who worked longer hours than I did, but
"wholesome example" was nowhere in their job descriptions.

When I dreamed about things that might make me more
whole, most of those dreams had no other people in them,
which made them seem a betrayal of parish ministry. I
dreamed of renting a cottage on a deserted beach and spending one whole week beyond the sound of another human
voice. I dreamed of taking a pile of books to a house in the
woods and reading one whole volume every day without inter-
ruption. I dreamed of living for a while in a town where I
knew no one and did not speak the language so I could go to
the store for butter or sit all night in a café without anyone

recognizing me. "Go into your cell," one of the Desert Fathers said, "and your cell will teach you everything." But I did not have a cell, and my increasing longing for one made me wonder whether I had taken a wrong turn somewhere.

By all accounts, loving God and my neighbor as myself was supposed to be enough to make me whole. I was in *Christian* ministry, after all. My own "wholesome example" was Christ, and when I looked at his life I did not see any beach cottages or all-night cafés. Instead, I saw someone who was always feeding people, healing people, teaching people, helping people. When he tried to withdraw from these people, they followed him. When they tried to eat him up, he did not resist. "Take, eat, this is my body, given for you," he said, holding out a loaf of challah to them. Like a single mother, he fed his spiritual offspring from his own flesh and blood until all of his reserves were gone. Then he died, and, though he rose from the dead three days later, this was quite an act to follow.

I did truly love helping people. It was not only chief among the reasons I had decided to seek ordination; it was also, I believed, why I had been born. To help lift a burden, to help light a path, to help heal a hurt, to help seek a truth — these struck me as the sorts of things that human beings were created to do for one another, and since church was one of the places where people went both to give and receive such help, I still believed that I was well placed. I just did not want to die. I wanted to get better, and I wanted the people I helped to get better too. Good, better, and best remained the operative categories for me, however, while the hunger for wholeness kept drilling holes in my heart.

It was during my tenure at All Saints' that I finally succeeded in raising a hurt bird to adulthood. I discovered the small, dark foundling under a bush in the church courtyard, cheeping for a mother who never came. When the baby finally gave up calling her and settled down to die, I scooped it up and took it home with me. For the next several weeks, I took it to work with me in a well-furnished shoebox, parking it on my desk as I answered telephone calls, planned schedules, and counseled couples preparing to be married. Every hour or so I got up to go microwave a couple of worms, having discovered that the main reason all my other baby birds had died was because I had not given them enough to eat.

Before long I was spending my lunch breaks driving far enough out of Atlanta to find bait shops that sold worms, but my dedication paid off. The brown baby grew into a sleek teenager with iridescent dark feathers and round black eyes, who greeted me with a screech in the morning and liked to sit on my head when I would let him. After a long session with the *Audubon Society Field Guide to North American Birds (Eastern Region)*, I finally deduced that I had raised a *Sturnus vulgaris*, otherwise known as a starling. This was something of a blow, since most people I knew thought starlings should be poisoned instead of fed, but I was so grateful to this bird for surviving under my care that I would have been happy to discover he was a turkey vulture.

I had come to think of him as a "he" by then, if only because of his raucous behavior. Having learned to fly, he made himself at home in my office, leaving his droppings on the windowsill, the back of my sofa, and occasionally my head. As much as I loved him, I knew it was time for him to go. In preparation for his release, I added live bugs and red berries to his diet, presenting the berries still attached to their leafy stems so that he would recognize them in the wild. He was so ravenous that I had no fear he would find plenty to eat on his own, but I still found reasons to delay his release. One day it would look like rain outside, and the next day he would look a little thin. What would I do without him to look after every day?

One sunny afternoon near the end of the sixth week, I decided not to take him home for the weekend. I would release him where I found him, near the same bush in the church courtyard. Maybe some of his kin were still hanging around and would show him the ropes. Maybe I would see him sometimes, even if I could not tell him from all the other starlings. Picking him up with one hand and cradling him against my body, I carried him outside. I told him how great his life was going to be while I stroked him for the last time, already seized with such tearful sorrow that I did not know if I could let him go. Then I opened my hand and he sprang into the air, flying so high, so fast, that I lost sight of him in a second.

*Well, that's that,* I thought, heading back into the church. Still teary, I packed up my briefcase and put the lid on the battered shoebox. I turned off the lights, locked the door, and walked down the stairs toward the parking lot, turning right at the last moment to take the long way through the courtyard. The place was deserted, of birds and of humans too. *Goodbye,* I said to the empty air, waiting a moment to see if anything stirred. When it did not, I turned my back and headed for the sidewalk. *Well, good,* I thought. *He's really gone, and that was the whole point, wasn't it?*

*To take care of him until he could take care of himself.* Then I heard a screech I recognized, but before I could turn back toward the courtyard to see where it had come from, I felt half a dozen bird toenails dig into my scalp. Baby was back, and it would take a second release deep in the woods of north Georgia before he flew away for good.

In years to come, I often thought of this as a parable of my life in the church. I had such a strong instinct for rescue that my breasts fairly leaked when I came across those in need of rescuing. Mother Church gave me a way to bring this instinct under God's roof. I took in as many fledglings as I could, fully intending to release them when they could fly, but the intimacy that developed between us made the releasing hard to do. Feeding others became my food. When they came back to dig their claws into my scalp, I took it as a compliment, at least until the flock had become so large that I could not hold my head up anymore.

When that time came, I decided that if the parable were true then God might be calling me to the woods of north Georgia again, where I could release the load I was carrying and take a second run at being both priest and whole.

Although the bishop had put my name on the list of nominees for Grace-Calvary, the rest was out of my hands. For close to a year, I waited while the search committee surveyed the congregation, composed a parish profile, and distributed it to potential candidates. As soon as I received my copy, I sent the updated résumé that I had already prepared. Some months after that, I learned that I had survived the final cut.

"A few of us want to hear you preach," the chair of the committee said over my home telephone as the blood started banging in my ears. "How soon can we come?"

She and I set a date. I produced a fulsome sermon. When the appointed Sunday arrived, I used all of my best grooming skills. I picked the cat hairs off my most expensive suit, smoothed my hair, and put a Band-Aid on the thumb I had chewed while working overtime on the sermon. Once I met the delegation at church I did my best to dazzle them, and after the service was over we sat for almost two hours in a Sunday school room as I answered question after question about my history, my beliefs, my weaknesses, and my strengths. One man on the committee noticed the Band-Aid on my thumb.

"What did you do to yourself?" he asked sympathetically.

"I cut it while I was cooking," I lied.

When my inquisitors finally climbed into their cars to drive home, I waved good-bye for what I supposed was the last time. I liked them. I even thought that I could love them, but I was sure that I was too urban for them, too anxious, too liberal, too tall. I was also a woman, which was a far larger problem in northeast Georgia than it was in Atlanta. When the chair of the committee finally called to ask me if I would come to Clarkesville, I could hear the weariness in her voice along with the elation. Months later I would learn how many families had left the church when they heard I was coming, and how much of their displeasure had been directed at her, but at the time all I learned was how pure bliss feels as it works its way from the flash of warmth in the feet to the fresh tingle in the scalp.

At my going-away party, the people of All Saints' showered me with gifts, including a quilt with many of their names stitched into its squares. Ed and I put our house on the market. We found a rental in Habersham County owned by a scion of the Fieldale chicken dynasty, with a barbecue grill big enough to cook two hundred chickens. We prepared to leave the city in which we had lived, both singly and together, for half our adult lives.

Abraham and Sarah were well into their seventies when they made their big move from Ur, packing up all they owned for destinations unknown. I was only forty and I knew exactly where I was going, but it was still such an act of faith that I was dizzy with fear when the time came to leave. Ed was at the wheel of our pickup truck, which was loaded with the last of our belongings. The sun was going down. Through the back window of the cab I could see bicycles, potted plants, suitcases, sacks of dog food, and a cooler with the contents of our refrigerator inside. There was also a green plastic garbage can full of dirt that Ed had heaved onto the bed of the truck at the last.

"You are taking *dirt?*" I asked him as we stood in the driveway.

"I am taking *compost,*" he answered, but of course it was more than that. Ed was not only taking the rich soil he had made from years of lawn clippings, scraped plates, and bags of leaves lifted from city curbs, he was also taking a sacrament of the quarter acre that he had loved for more than a decade. On it sat the house to which he had added a whole room for my books before we were married, the same house in which we spent our wedding night. Every summer, in the small rectangle of full sun out back, he had planted green beans that took over the wooden rail of the deck. He had ringed the mailbox out front with broccoli plants and sowed cherry tomato seeds where our more refined neighbors would have preferred to see purple phlox. While those same neighbors brought their produce home in tan plastic bags, Ed presented me with split oak baskets full of fresh lettuce, arugula, and chard. Moving to the country was as much his idea as mine, but he was not going without his dirt.

When he turned the wheel of the pickup hard to the left on our way out of the driveway, a piece of lumber wedged in the bed smashed against the back window of the cab, so that my last view of our old house was through shattered glass. I thought I should cry but I was too tired, so I turned around and stared straight ahead instead. I am sure that Ed and I spoke during the next hour and a half, but I do not remember what we said. What I remember is how the light changed.

At first the view through the windshield was as bright as a runway at the airport. There were street lights, headlights, shop lights, stoplights. Even at night the city sky was a tarnished copper color, with flashing lights atop microwave towers and tall office buildings beating out their different pulses all along the skyline. As we passed the grocery store, nighthawks swooped through the air above lit billboards catching bugs, while shoppers loaded their food into their trunks under a small forest of mercury vapor lights. An oncoming car flashed its brights at us, and Ed clicked ours down. Then we turned onto the expressway and joined the river of headlights flowing north.

For the next thirty miles we watched the light show taking place all around us. While one scrolling sign provided us with the time and temperature, another promised us a hotel room for the special AARP rate of $39.95. The blue lights of a police car on the right shoulder of the eight-lane road lit our faces before the red lights of an ambulance sped by us on the left. Up above, the Golden Arches shone brighter than the signs for Cracker Barrel, Taco Bell, or Burger King, but not as bright as the spotlighted miniature blimp that floated above the Subaru dealership. More scrolling signs over the highway alerted us to road work ahead with increased fines for speeding, while lit billboards on either side offered to meet our needs for everything from personal injury lawyers to spirit-filled churches where we would be welcomed as family.

When the perimeter highway circling Atlanta was first built, it was the boundary between city and countryside. When Ed and I crossed under it in the spring of 1992, we were still well inside the greater metro-Atlanta area, but the psychological barrier remained intact. We might as well have been crossing the Mississippi in the late 1800s for all that we knew about life on the other side. The town we were moving to had two stoplights and no women clergy. The only movie theater in the county was nine miles away. The chicken industry drove the local economy, and the lay leader of the congregation I was going to raised pigs. He was also a Georgia Tech graduate who flew his own plane and drove a Volvo, but even he admitted that Clarkesville was a long way from Atlanta.

This may help explain the wave of nausea that rolled through me as the lights of the city vanished in the rearview mirror. While it was true that I had gotten exactly what I wanted, it was not until the sky turned black that I physically registered how much I was leaving behind: home, family, familiarity, security. When we got where we were going, I would not even be able to find the bathroom light switch in the dark. The cab of that truck was my spaceship, the one safe place I could think of to be, even as it carried me beyond all safety. Would I be able to breathe when I got where I was going, or would I float gasping into outer space before I wrenched free of this vivid dream?

Thirty minutes out of Atlanta, Ed took the exit that led north to Clarkesville. Except for one set of red taillights in the distance, the view through the windshield was entirely dark. The growl of our engine was the only sound we heard. I stretched my arm across the bench seat and put my hand on the worn denim above Ed's knee.

"Music?" he asked.

"Sure," I said, but when I turned on the radio our favorite station was full of static. I spent the next ten minutes searching for something other than country music and Christian evangelism on the dial, but those were the two main choices. Adding Linda Wertheimer and Noah Adams to my growing list of losses, I made a mental note. *Never move anywhere that does not have a public radio station.* Then I found a Willie Nelson tape in the glove compartment and put him in charge of easing our transition into the world of his songs.

As Willie crooned about honky-tonk bars and family Bibles, I began to see details in the dark. A thin line of deepest blue separated the treetops from the night sky. Bright specks of light, always paired, shone out of the grasses along the shoulder of the road. The short ones turned out to be mostly cats and the tall ones all deer. As our high beams swept past them, I could see them raise their heads to point their ears at our bright specks of light, also paired.

Every now and then I would see a glow in the sky ahead, like a distant volcano burping light. As we drew nearer I could see that it was a convenience store instead, with half a dozen gas pumps outside and so many lights that a surgeon could have operated right there on a car hood. To look directly at those lights was to be hit in the head with a pain between the eyes, so I learned to look away instead. After the third store I kept my eyes closed for a while, and when I opened them again the view through the windshield was thick with stars.

It was not as if I had never seen stars before. Even in the city, I could sometimes see the big stars on a clear night: Jupiter, Venus, the Big Dipper. But it had been a long time since I had seen the stars between the stars, a virtual curtain of stardust upon which the larger constellations were hung. When Ed stopped the truck so we could admire them without a windshield in the way, we saw something else that we had previously accepted chiefly on hearsay. The stars actually *twinkled*. With no yellow sulfur haze between them and us, they looked less like steady ten-watt bulbs and more like diamonds being turned on black flannel under a bright lamp. They changed colors as the light flashed out from them, first blue, then gold, then rose. They danced in place with such energy that I swear I heard them rustling—or was that the breeze in the ten thousand breathing leaves?

The roar of the truck engine drowned them out, but when I looked out the shattered back window of the cab, I no longer saw what I was leaving behind. Instead, I saw what Abraham and Sarah must have seen: a night sky that went on forever, under which my small sorrow was already turning to awe.

# CHAPTER
## 6

Later that same week, the moving van pulled away from the parish house in a burst of diesel exhaust. As the sound died away, I plumped the cushion on my desk chair and sat down. Like the rest of my office furniture, the chair was still outside on the sidewalk, under an oak so old and enchanted looking that I half expected it to lean down and speak. From where I sat beneath its sheltering arms, I had a postcard view of Grace-Calvary Episcopal Church, aka My New Church.

Suspended for one liquid morning between the dreaming and the coming true, I tried not to think about how much anxiety my selection had caused. The Episcopal Church had been ordaining women to priesthood for almost sixteen years by that time, but women in charge of congregations remained rare. In Clarkesville, where many local churches still taught that scripture forbade women to speak in church, my arrival confirmed what many already suspected about Episcopalians. When one teenager's mother broke the news to her, the girl wailed out loud, "God, Mom, people already think we're so

weird—do we have to have a woman too?" Several families left
the church before I arrived, and others were poised to leave. I
knew that I would drive myself crazy if I thought about it too
much, so I followed the protocol that I had established during
my previous years in ordained ministry. I got up out of the
chair and went to work.

I do not know how male clergy begin their new jobs, but I
begin mine by cleaning. That first week I cleaned windows,
cleaned files, cleaned closets and cupboards. When I finished
with my study and the parish house kitchen, I proceeded to the
church library, where new shelves had been built to hold all of
Julian's old books. Among them I found a cache of nineteenth-
century prayer books that I assumed he had collected, at least
until I saw "Grace Church 1854" written inside one of the
front covers in faded brown ink. There were ghosts all over the
place, but most of them were friendly.

One morning I arrived to find a vase full of yellow daffodils
and a quilted jar of muscadine jelly in front of my door. Another morning there were two pastel flowered napkins inside
carved wooden napkin rings with a note that said, "Welcome
home, Barbara and Ed." As the week wore on, parishioners
showed up both to help me get settled and to do their own
jobs, which included everything from weeding the garden to
polishing the silver. Charlotte hung the new curtains that she
had made to go with the upholstery on my old cane-back sofa
while her husband, Stan, turned one whole wall of my study
into bookshelves. Gil walked me through the labyrinth of
church finance and administration. Noreen invited me to the
weekly meeting of the Daughters of the King, where I met

women who took prayer as seriously as other people take breathing. John showed me around the small kitchen in the parish house, where he routinely turned five bags of groceries and two pounds of chicken into a feast for, if not thousands, then at least everyone who showed up for a Wednesday night supper.

One quiet afternoon near the end of the week, I came back from lunch to find a slight, sandy-haired man arranging flowers in the kitchen. They were mostly roses, but not the tight, scentless kind you buy at the grocery store. These had the ripe, opulent look of roses plucked from an English garden. Their scent drenched the air. Since the man was intent on what he was doing, I did not introduce myself right away. Instead I leaned against the counter and watched him work.

"You're good at that," I said after a couple of minutes. He picked up a dusky rose and considered where to put it. When he found the place, he took up a pair of clippers and snipped the stem to the right length, angling it at the end so that it would enter the green florist's block like an arrow.

"Why don't I like women priests?" he said, with his back still to me, as he jabbed the stem into place. I took a breath. *En garde.*

"I don't know," I said. "Why don't you?"

"I don't know either," he said, holding another rose the way a painter holds a paintbrush — straight out from his nose, sighting his next stroke. "I just don't."

"I'm Barbara," I said.

"I know who you are, Mrs. Taylor," he said. "My name is Bruce." I cannot remember if he ever turned around, but I do remember taking an instant liking to him. He not only was a genius with flowers, he was also genuine with me. Even if his genuine disapproval was my first experience of this, I knew that I would not have to spend a lot of time trying to guess what Bruce thought about me or anything else. He was a straight shooter, with a quirky nineteenth-century kind of courtesy that made me think he might aim for my shoulder and not my heart.

As I would soon discover, he was among the people who missed Saint Julian most. Because I was so happy to be at Grace-Calvary, I often forgot how many in the congregation were still grieving his death. Instead of lessening their sense of loss, my arrival had deepened it, since the presence of a new rector was the surest reminder that the old rector was really gone. As I paid calls on parishioners those first few weeks, I watched their faces soften as they remembered the Friday nights when Julian would show up, unannounced, to invite himself to supper — and would fall asleep on the couch afterward so that they had to shake him awake when it was time for them to go to bed. I also heard stories about how pissy he could be, especially from the pulpit, where he found ways to work his grievances with various parishioners into his Sunday sermons. "He was the only man I knew who had permanent PMS," one woman said with unmistakable affection.

Because Julian was a single man in a small town, some of his parishioners were also his best friends. One of them told me how he and Julian used to spend Julian's day off paddling a canoe down the Chattahoochee River, working their way through a cold six-pack. Another told me how Julian had taken him into the rectory, offering him a free place to live while he pulled his life back together. While such stories gave me even more to admire about Julian, they also increased my dread of following him. I had come to Clarkesville with a husband I really liked, who was my first choice for roommate as well as for company on my nights and days off. I had also come with a resolution to lighten the load on my head by keeping as many birds in the air as I could.

One afternoon after the parish secretary had gone home, I was sitting in my new office admiring the view out my four windows when I heard the sound of distant car horns honking. As the horns drew nearer, I realized that I was hearing not cars in town but Canada geese overhead, flying directly over the roof of the parish house. Their wild calls had so much life in them, so much hollering breath and direction, that my own breath came more quickly just hearing them. I could not have asked for more blessed assurance that my life had really changed. The sounds outside my windows were no longer car horns and traffic helicopters but migrating geese. Like them, I had left my old home when all the food was gone, following my instinct to a new, green place where I hoped to regain my strength for ministry. Also like them, I did not know where my flight plan had come from, but I trusted that the Divine Presence was mixed up in it somehow.

Clarkesville was so compact that I began walking to the post office to pick up the mail every day. One day I would take the route that led past the old town cemetery and the next day the one that went by the public library. On my second trip past the library, I turned around, went inside, and walked out five minutes later with a laminated library card in my pocket. When the *Northeast Georgian* published my picture over a brief article about Grace-Calvary's new minister, my privileges around town increased. The owner of Dixie Gallery offered me a 10 percent clergy discount on antiques. The manager of Woods Furniture Store invited me to give the weekly devotional for her sales staff. Back at the post office, the clerk told me not to worry when I came up a quarter short on a book of stamps. "Just bring it back before we close at five," she said, sliding my stamps across the counter to me with a smile.

Of course people also knew where I got my hair cut, what I served my dinner guests on Friday night, and how fast I drove on the four-lane highway. The anonymity of my life in the city was over, along with many of the professional boundaries that had gone with it. One church member said he could help me find some better-tailored clothes while another offered to wash the red Georgia dirt off my truly filthy car. When I tried to enlist the parish secretary's help in teaching people to make appointments if they wanted to see me, she gently explained that most of them did not keep day planners like I did. "If they want to see you then they'll stop by," Marty said, "and if you're busy then they'll come back later." Meanwhile, she added, there were some people I might want to visit at home. Would I like her to make up a list for me?

In this way I began to learn what it meant to be a parson— a representative person—whose every move reflected upon her parishioners. By the time my first Sunday arrived, I was so anxious that I vibrated from head to foot. I had produced a painfully overworked sermon with three points in it that all started with a *p.* I had washed and ironed my vestments. At ten minutes before the hour, the tiny sacristy was full of people — acolytes, lay readers, altar guild members, and Skip, the semiretired physician from Florida who served as deacon at Grace-Calvary. It was almost time for us to head to the front porch of the church for the processional when everyone got quiet and looked at me. I wondered if I had something on my face and they were all waiting to see who would tell me. Then I remembered that I was the rector and they were all waiting for me to pray.

I prayed. We headed to the porch, where we stood with the ushers while the last few worshipers climbed the steps and went inside. When the head usher looked at me for the signal to ring the bell, I nodded, and the sky above all our heads erupted with sound. The first chord of the first hymn burst out the doors of the church as the procession entered them. Since I was rector, my place was not at the front of the line but at the end. This prevented me from remembering what a small place Grace-Calvary was until I stepped inside. The walk from the door to the altar took all of five seconds, which left quite a lot of the hymn to sing. When it was over, I stepped to the center of the altar rail and spread my hands, feeling as I imagine some women must feel after they have given birth. After so much waiting, so much worrying, and so much labor, both physical and emotional, I was looking into the faces of the people I had chosen to love.

"Blessed be God: Father, Son, and Holy Spirit," I said to them.

"And blessed be his kingdom," they replied, "now and for ever. Amen."

If I had hoped for a little less of the leaking breast syn-drome at Grace-Calvary, that hope was already dashed. My sense of ownership was staggering, in spite of the fact that I had just arrived. The smallness of the congregation would have triggered my protectiveness even without my awareness of their grief, but that awareness kicked me into even higher gear. Like the second wife of a widower, I wanted to make up for what they had lost when Julian died, without trying to take his place. By the end of the first month I felt responsible for ev-erything from the happiness of the babies in the nursery to the cleanliness of the windows in the church. If this proved exhil-arating instead of exhausting to me, that was not only because I was finally in charge of my own congregation but also be-cause I found that congregation so worth my while.

While the church directory listed almost five hundred names, the two hundred and fifty people who actually showed up to have their pictures taken provided a more accurate count. They included college professors, real estate agents, shop owners, and artists plus a whole flock of retirees from Florida. In a big city they might have found homes in five markedly different parishes, but in a county with only one Episcopal church they learned to live together — the Yellow Dog Democrats, the National Rifle Association boosters, the Daughters of the American Revolution, and the League of Women Voters. Once, when I asked a newcomer what had brought him to Grace-Calvary, he shook his head. "I know people who come to this church," he said, "and I finally had to come see for myself how they got through a Sunday morning without assaulting each other."

Far from assaulting each other, they seemed as intrigued as I was by their differences. People who canceled out one another's votes in every county election cooked soup together at the Clarkesville Soup Kitchen. Champions of the decommissioned 1928 Book of Common Prayer attended Sunday school with charismatics who prayed with both hands in the air. When the British-born lector stood to announce a reading from the prophet I-*zigh*-ah, Southerners who used verb constructions such as "I might could have done that" sighed with pleasure, and when the auto mechanic in charge of the church softball team needed more players, he recruited the economist with the PhD.

When my friends in Atlanta asked me how things were going in north Georgia, I told them that I was living in a Flannery O'Connor story. I would spend one afternoon visiting a septuagenarian who lived in an octagonal house that her late husband had built for her, eating kiwis that she grew on her clothesline and listening to her reminiscences of Isadora Duncan. The next day I would take communion to a man who was back in the hospital for the third operation on his knee, which was crushed when his pickup truck rolled backward and pinned him against his trailer. After church on Trinity Sunday, I came out to my car to find a miniature Three Musketeers candy bar on the hood. Underneath it was a note from the deeply eccentric woman who lived across the street from the church. "One for all and all for one," the note read. "Happy Trinity Sunday."

Since clergy are bound to protect the confidences we keep, I cannot tell most of the stories that made Grace-Calvary such a colorful place to be. I cannot go into detail about the Italian chef whom I bailed out of jail or the two vestrymen who got into such a fight one Monday night that one of them had to lie down on the couch with chest pains while we finished the meeting. But there were other characters around town who had told their own stories so often that the details were common knowledge.

One local mother-and-daughter team had been coming to Grace-Calvary for money since long before I arrived. I never knew if they were churchgoers themselves, but they knew their way around the county churches better than the Chamber of Commerce did. The grown daughter was allegedly diabetic, and the elderly mother routinely called for things that were not available from the community food bank, such as sugar-free chewing gum, cookies, cakes, candy, canned fruit, fruit juices, soft drinks, pudding mixes, ice cream, and pancake syrup.

Every couple of months these two did something that put them on probation at the food bank, which meant that they really did run short on staples from time to time. When I believed that such a time had come, I bought them some groceries, which kept me near the top of the mother's calling list. Even when I said no, she took this not as discouragement but as a challenge to try harder.

"Martha is sitting on the toilet and we are out of toilet paper," she told me on the telephone one afternoon. "If I came over right now, could you write me a check to the grocery store so she can get up?"

I also spent time with people I never saw again. One afternoon after everyone else had gone home I answered a knock at the door of the parish house, opening it to a ravaged looking young man who said he needed help getting home to North Carolina. He was taller than I was, with a recently shaved head of hair that was growing out at different speeds. Still acting on my lifelong and generally mistaken notion that most people want to be listened to as much as they want money, I asked him to come inside and tell me his story.

He shuffled inside and sat down in my office, pushing up the sleeves of his oily jacket so that I could see the scars on the inside of his arms. Then he told me about how he had just been released from the state hospital at Milledgeville and was trying to find some cousins of his who used to live in North Carolina. He needed to find them pretty fast too, he said, because he was out of everything, including the pills that the people at the hospital had given him when he left. When he started digging around in his pants pocket to find the slip of paper with his diagnosis on it, I gave him thirty-five dollars in cash and wished him luck.

After working so many years in Atlanta, I had to learn how to work in a town with no Traveler's Aid office, no Salvation Army, no homeless shelter or poverty law office. There were no counseling centers either, but the few local people I knew who were in therapy said they would rather drive a hundred miles round-trip than be seen coming out of a therapist's office in town, which explained that. When people in Habersham County got into truly terrible trouble, they went to the emergency room or the fire station. When they thought they had a little more time they went to a church, where they hoped to find someone more skilled than they were at getting God's attention.

During my first year at Grace-Calvary, I talked with scores of people suffering from addiction, eviction, physical abuse, incest, bankruptcy, multiple personality disorder, depression, and AIDS, only about half of whom were members of the church. I not only learned that my new job involved caring for people who were not in the picture directory, I also learned that Clarkesville had a shadow side I had not seen from the sunny front porch of Grace-Calvary Church.

There may not have been homeless people sleeping in the bushes, but there were poor, illiterate, and mentally ill people living in trailer parks. There were unmarried teenage girls with two babies by different fathers buying formula with food stamps while their brothers got blind drunk on Friday nights as compensation for another week of backbreaking work at minimum wage. There were Laotian, Vietnamese, and Mexican immigrants moving to town for entry-level jobs at the chicken plant, and there were old-fashioned white supremacists who suddenly had a whole new crowd threatening their supremacy.

On my first January in Clarkesville, the Northeast Georgia Peace Council invited me to join other local clergy at the head of the annual Martin Luther King Jr. Peace Walk. When I arrived at the starting point to accept this honor, the place was crawling with police cars, photographers, and newspaper reporters. They all but outnumbered the walkers, who were huddled together trying to keep warm while they waited for enough people to begin.

"What's with the police?" I asked a woman with a red scarf wrapped around her neck. She did not look like the type to break store windows or set dumpsters on fire.

"Oh, they're here in case the Klan shows up," she said, as I felt the hairs on the back of my neck spring up. Eventually I found two other clergy and waited with them for the rest of the Habersham Ministerial Association to show up. When the walk finally began, there were still just three of us: the white Presbyterian pastor, the black Baptist minister, and me. As we faced the photographers and the police, I realized that what I had construed as an honor was more like a safety feature for the small crowd behind us. The three of us in front were human air bags in case of collision with the Klan.

We were singing "He's Got the Whole World in His Hands" when we headed up the small hill toward the Clarkesville square, which was where we saw them. Three men in white robes and peaked hoods stood on the curb with police on both sides of them while some women and children with greasy hair sat heaped in a beat-up van behind them. One man held a sign that said, "James Earl Ray made my day." Another held a picture of Dr. King's face with a rifle target on his forehead.

To my surprise, I could see their faces too. The Klansmen were wearing their hoods but not the masks with the spooky eyeholes, so that I got a good look at all three of them. What I saw was so empty, so stone-cold vacant, that I was not afraid of them anymore. They were just people, as scared and lost looking as anyone. "He's got you and me, brother, in his hands," I sang as we turned the corner and left them behind. "He's got you and me, sister, in his hands." It was the nicest thing I could

think of to say to them, and what is more, I believed it was
true.

To be honest, that was one of the more dramatic things that
ever happened in Clarkesville. Day by day, I did what most
clergy do. I proofread the mailed bulletin, answered the telephone, chose the hymns for Sunday, and changed the lightbulb
in the bathroom. I sat with families in the waiting room at the
hospital and spooned applesauce into the mouths of patients
at the nursing home. I visited shut-ins at home as well as a few
at the county jail. I learned how to send money orders and
post bond. I gave the invocation at the Special Olympics held
in the high school football stadium and ate lunch at the
Clarkesville Soup Kitchen with some of the regulars. I taught
Sunday school, counseled couples, wrote annual reports, and
led worship.

I also learned the difference between being an assistant to
the rector and the rector, the main difference being that when
I looked around for clergy support, I was the only person
there. I had become the one church members called when they
landed in the emergency room or found a loved one lying lifeless on the bathroom floor. I also had become the one they
called when they were furious about the way the finance committee was investing the church endowment or the way a Sunday school teacher had spoken to a child or the way the
Episcopal Church was treating gay people.

In seminary I had read about the phenomenon of transference, whereby human beings sometimes transfer the feelings
they have for one pivotal person in their lives to another pivotal person in their lives, especially when they are feeling vul-

nerable in a relationship. I had read about it, but I had never gotten a full dose of what it meant until I was the sole pastor of a church. Sometimes, when people were busy adoring me or despising me, I got the distinct impression that it was not about me at all. I reminded them of someone else who was no longer around but who had made such a large dent in their lives that they were still trying to work it out. In a church where male clergy are often referred to as Father, I should not have been surprised that some people thought of me as Mother, especially since I had already recognized that dynamic from my side. What did surprise me was the depth of feeling I could evoke in people by doing a small kindness on the one hand or botching a small detail on the other. Once, when I sent a card to a new church member without remembering that she used her maiden name instead of her husband's, I received such a hostile telephone call from her that I felt stunned for the better part of an hour.

The real problem with transference for clergy without the skills to deal with it is that it feeds our sense that we are more powerful than we really are. While I was still trying to find someone who could teach me these skills, I had a hard time saying no to those who believed I had the power to help them, even when what they wanted me to do seemed futile to me. When they asked me to call on unchurched friends of theirs in the hospital, I went although I knew that those poor people had no interest in seeing me. When they asked me to talk to their rebellious teenagers, I did so even when I believed that the rebellion was in order. I even prayed for one couple to find water on the property where they hoped to build a house, although I did not believe that God was in the well-drilling business. When another couple came out of church one Sunday morning and asked me if I could arrange good weather for a family picnic that afternoon, I drew the line. "Sorry, but I don't do weather," I said. "I'm a priest, not a witch."

When they came out of church the following Sunday and thanked me for arranging the good weather, I had fresh occasion to wonder whether my priesthood was mine to define at all. It was not "my" priesthood, of course. It was Christ's priesthood, in which the church allowed me to participate, but there were days when I wondered what Jesus would have done if he had been called upon to recognize graduating seniors in church, prepare an annual report for the bishop, or speak for fifteen minutes over chicken-fried steak to the Rotary Club. In his absence, I was called upon to do so many things that seemed to have nothing to do with the worship of God that I began to envy specialists like my father the psychotherapist, who could say things such as, "I'm sorry, but our time is up now," or "I wish I could help you, but my client load is full."

On my worst nights I lay in bed feeling like a single parent, unable to sleep because I knew I did not have enough love in me to go around. God was the boundless lover, but for many people God was the parent who had left. They still read about him in the Bible and sang about him in hymns. They still believed in his reality, which made it even harder to accept his apparent lack of interest in them. They waited for messages from him that did not arrive. They prepared their hearts for meetings that never happened. They listened to other Christians speak as if God showed up every night for supper, leaving them to wonder what they had done wrong to make God go off and start another family.

I suppose I could have helped them see how their life histories deepened their distress or given them some more grown-up ways of conceiving of God, but few were interested in that. We were engaged in a more ancient drama, wrestling far more primitive fears. Because I was wedded to the One who was gone, I stood in for him. I took many of the blows intended for him and received much of the adulation. I kept the old stories about him alive and told some new ones as proof of his ongoing vitality. I blessed, fed, and forgave the children in his name, reassuring them that their fears were ungrounded and their hopes well placed. The unspoken deal, I think, was that as long as I did this, no one would openly question God's love or existence. As long as I filled in, no one would ask where God was or why he was not more attentive.

In my case, the attention deficit was all mine. I had moved to the country in order to lie down in more blessed fields, to live closer to the Divine Presence that had held me all my life, but I had once again become so busy caring for the household of God that I neglected the One who had called me there. If I still had plenty of energy for the work, that was because feeding others was still my food. As long as I fed them, I did not feel my hunger pains.

*7*

After six months in a rental home that was too large for us, Ed and I began looking for land to buy. Our search for an old farmhouse had run into a snag since everything that went by that description really was a *farm* house, with chicken houses out back, a falling-down barn littered with broken machinery, and muddy pastures full of cows. We even looked at one place with its own hog shed before deciding that we would build our own new, old farmhouse if only we could find the right piece of land.

Ed's requirement was that the land have running water on it. Mine was that we live no farther than ten miles from town. For the next year and a half we trekked all over the county, finding property that met one requirement but not the other. I ruined a great pair of Cole Haan shoes walking river property with strange humps all over it, which turned out to be old pits from an early mica-mining operation. We looked at mountain property that had been clear-cut, leaving tooth-shaped holes in the ridgeline. We found a heavenly piece of land with rolling pastures and a fast-running stream that was almost twenty miles from town as well as a striking knoll just four miles out of town that had not a drop of water on it, but after all our looking we had not discovered a single piece of land that one of us did not disqualify within five minutes of setting foot on it.

Then one day Ed said that he had met a man who was selling off some of his own pastureland for what sounded like a decent price. We could buy almost a hundred acres with what we had saved from the sale of our quarter acre in Atlanta. Unrolling the county map that he kept stashed in the trunk of his car, Ed pointed to a large white space with no roads in it near the northwest edge of the county. "See this?" he said, running his finger along a thin blue line. "Stream. And this?" he said, caressing another. "Stream." All in all, three streams crossed the land, converging on their way to the nearby Chattahoochee River. As tired as I was of being disappointed, I pulled on my rubber boots, got into the car, and set the trip meter to zero.

Following the directions Ed had been given, we drove well out of town, passing one gas station, one barbecue stand, and four churches along the way. "Eating forbidden fruit makes many jams," read one church sign. "Give Satan an inch and he will become your ruler," read another. Leaving the pavement, we turned down one dirt road and then another, as a huge cloud of red dust fanned out behind us. I counted seven houses over the next mile and half, including one log cabin and one Christmas tree farm, before the road ended at a red metal farm gate. The trip meter said nine miles even.

Ed and I parked the car in a clump of scrub pines, lifted the heavy chain that held the gate shut, and walked onto the land under the spread limbs of an old white oak. As I stepped from its shadow into the full light of morning, I looked up to see green flowing in every direction. The land rolled like a silk sheet in a big wind, with matching hills on either side of a valley that wound out of sight. While the tops of the hills were bare of trees, their flanks held dark patches of woods where I could see brown cows switching their tails in the shade. The word *copse* came suddenly to mind, a word I had read in poems but had never seen in person. The flanks of the hills were covered with copses, and the very sight of them softened me.

Some people spend years of their lives searching for the person whom they were born to love. I spent close to two searching for the land where I was meant to live. After scores of failed blind dates, I decided to marry the land that day, before I had walked ten steps past the oak—before I had found the trillium and the jewelweed, before the elderberry had produced its tiny purple clusters or the persimmon had dropped its plump fruit on the ground. I fell in love before I ever plucked a ripe muscadine from the vine or made a pie from the blackberries that grow along the path to the river. The milkweed was still in its pod that day, but even if I had seen it spilling its white silk on the air, my heart needed no more convincing. I had found my place on earth.

I know plenty of people who find God most reliably in books, in buildings, and even in other people. I have found God in all of these places too, but the most reliable meeting place for me has always been creation. Since I first became aware of the Divine Presence in that lit-up field in Kansas, I have known where to go when my own flame is guttering. To lie with my back flat on the fragrant ground is to receive a transfusion of the same power that makes the green blade rise. To remember that I am dirt and to dirt I shall return is to be given my life back again, if only for one present moment at a time. Where other people see acreage, timber, soil, and river frontage, I see God's body, or at least as much of it as I am able to see. In the only wisdom I have at my disposal, the Creator does not live apart from creation but spans and suffuses it. When I take a breath, God's Holy Spirit enters me. When a cricket speaks to me, I talk back. Like everything else on earth, I am an embodied soul, who leaps to life when I recognize my kin. If this makes me a pagan, then I am a grateful one.

I *know* I am Irish, which may explain a lot. When I first visited the Emerald Isle several years ago, my gene pool told me I was home. It was not just the freckles and the fondness for potatoes that convinced me, but the natural reverence for creation that I found in that blessed land. From the Dingle Peninsula to the Skellig Islands, I encountered holy rocks, holy caves, holy pools, and holy groves. I learned the proper name for those places on earth where the Presence is so strong that they serve as portals between this world and another. "Thin places," the Irish call them, which turn out to include not only the famous places such as Croagh Patrick and Glendalough but also the ordinary places that people walk right by if they are not paying attention.

On our first day in Ireland, Ed and I discovered a thin place in a cow pasture. We were not looking for it. We were just taking a walk down a country lane after supper when we saw a break in the hedges off to our left, like a hole in a garden wall. Curious, we followed the well-worn footpath a couple of hundred feet to where it ended at a little mossy hole full of crystal clear water. If not for the tidy bank of stones set into its side, we might have mistaken it for an ordinary watering hole, but someone had clearly taken pains to hallow the place.

"Do you feel that?" Ed said.

"I do," I said. Freshness was pouring from that spring, drenching me as thoroughly as a shower. I felt as peaceful and alive as I had felt in ages. My jet lag was all gone. How it worked was a complete mystery to me, but there was no denying the effect. Simply to stand near that spring was to experience living water.

Later I would find the Celtic theology that went with the experience, in which God's "big book" of creation is revered alongside God's "little book" of sacred scripture. I would also find Christian mystics such as Bernard of Clairvaux and Julian of Norwich, who found heaven on earth in union with the Divine. "I have had no other masters than the beeches and the oaks," Bernard wrote in the twelfth century, while Julian recognized the love of God in a hazel nut in her hand. Hildegard of Bingen coined the word *viriditas* ("green power") to describe the divine power of creation, while Francis of Assisi composed love songs to Brother Sun and Sister Moon.

"You never enjoy the world aright till the sea itself floweth in your veins," wrote the seventeenth-century Anglican priest Thomas Traherne, "till you are clothed with the heavens and crowned with the stars; and perceive yourself to be the sole heir of the whole world, and more than so, because men are in

it who are every one sole heirs as well as you."* Since I had received Christian education that taught me to view creation as
both fallen and inert, I was happy to discover these dissenting
opinions, but they only confirmed what I already knew to be
true. I did not live on the earth but in it, in communion with
all that gave me life.

"Just wait," Ed said back in Georgia, leading me around the
thin place he had found. When we reached the top of the first
hill, he turned me around to see Mount Yonah in the fore-
ground, with its great face of exposed rock barely visible to the
west, and rounder Pink Mountain just behind. Below and all
around those two peaks, all I saw were the tops of trees, without a roof line, a telephone pole, or a microwave tower in sight.
After we had sat long enough to hear the shushing of the river
a quarter mile away, we headed down the far slope toward a
stream shooting sparks through the trees.

Before we got there, Ed led me under a canopy of leaves toward a pool of water so dark with tannin that I could not see
the bottom. Hidden frogs croaked once as we approached and
then leapt into the water. By the time I arrived all I saw were
ripples. The largest of three springs on the property, this one
produced a steady stream of water that came out through the
roots of a big poplar tree. "We could dig it out and cap it for
our water," Ed said.

"Or we could leave it alone," I said, already feeling protective of the land. I was used to feeling that way about living

---

*Quoted in Aldous Huxley, *The Perennial Philosophy* (New York: Harper & Row,
1945), 67.

things, but for the first time in my life I was feeling maternal toward a place. I wanted to evict the cows that were eroding the banks of the spring. I wanted to remove the strands of rusty barbed wire that were embedded in the trunks of the trees along the creek. I wanted to collect the empty beer cans left by careless hunters and banish those trespassers from the land forever if they could not pick up after themselves any better than that. No one had to explain to me why Mother Nature was a she.

The spring emptied into a creek that we followed for ten minutes or more, past banks of blackberry bushes just beginning to green up for the summer and dead pines still standing with great holes pecked in them by the pileated woodpeckers I had already heard in the woods. All of a sudden there was a great commotion just ahead of us. Stopping to locate the source of it, I watched a great blue heron lift off from the creek, with stick legs still trailing in the water as the massive wings beat and then folded just in time to escape through the awning of the trees. When I could breathe again, we continued past where one creek joined another to the flood plain near the west end of the property, clearly a favorite grazing spot for the cows.

Since the creek continued toward the river on someone else's land, we took the overland route, hiking up and over the ridge toward the sound of rushing water on the other side. Following a deer trail most of the way, we got as close to the sound as we could. Then we pushed our way through a stand of mountain laurel that was twice as tall as we were and teetered on the bank of the Chattahoochee, watching a pair of wood ducks we had just startled flying away from us up the river. Ten feet below, a huge stone jutted out into the river, flat enough to stand on. Hanging on to branches of mountain laurel, we lowered ourselves down to it and stood surrounded by wild river on three sides.

Seventy-five miles south of where we stood, the Chattahoochee was a broad, brown river foaming with suds that ran through the suburbs of Atlanta. When I lived there, I knew a particular subdivision that included a small park on the river, where I could go when I needed to be near living water. To enjoy the view, I had to ignore the crushed Styrofoam cups spiraling with other trash in the shallows as well as the plastic grocery bags hung in the branches nearest the water. I had to overlook the old tire halfway buried in the small river beach and the dead fish lying next to it, not to mention the decks, landings, lawn furniture, barbecue grills, and bird feeders that pocked the river's edge.

From where I stood, I could not see a sign of human occupation. Like a child who has not yet dodged a blow, the river in front of me was innocent of what lay ahead. The water was so clear I could see a lazy carp paddling below me. The only debris was a high-water mark made of small sticks and leaves. There were raccoon tracks in the sand where the rock met the riverbank and white splats on the stone where some big water bird had stopped to fish for a spell.

"How long do you think this river has been here?" I asked Ed. When he did not answer, I tried out answers of my own. Since the mountains were made? Since the first rains fell? Since the earth cooled?

"Forever, I guess," he said at last. If I softened my gaze and stopped holding myself apart from all that surrounded me, I became part of something so old and so powerfully alive that I lost track of my self. The river ran through me. Trees breathed for me. My feet grew from rock. The only thing wrong with any of these sentences is that there was for that moment no "me" or "my." I lost my "me" altogether, which of course was not apparent until I came back to my self, recovering one sense of reality at the price of the other.

When we had received the river's blessing, Ed and I headed up the hill through the woods toward the old county road, where we found the first graves on the highest ridge. The piles of stones were miles from the famous Indian mound in White County. Most of them had been plundered long ago, but both their east-west orientation and the stones placed at cardinal points around their edges told us that we were walking through an old burial ground. This was no real surprise, since the land had felt sacred from the moment we set foot on it. Water was plentiful, the river was thick with fish, and the level floodplain was perfect for a small settlement. We did not need to check the county records to guess that we were on old Cherokee land.

By the time we returned to our car, we had named the place Indian Ridge Farm. All that remained was to haggle with the owner over the price — and to decide which hill would be the site of our new home.

The announcement that we had bought land was welcomed at church, where it served as a sign of our intention to stay put. Once Ed and I had chosen a builder, a blueprint, and a flat spot to build, we asked a couple of members with construction savvy to come help us site our house. While Ed and John talked about where the driveway should go, I walked Bob up the steps of my imaginary mudroom into my imaginary kitchen.

"I want the window *here* so I can see the mountains while I'm washing dishes," I said.

"I understand that," Bob said, "but there is only one way your house is going to fit on this hill, and that's not it." The kitchen vanished. We were standing in a cow pasture again. Bob leaned over the blueprint of the house, traced the footprint with his finger, and led me around the hilltop counting off paces as he went.

"You see?" he said. "It won't fit." I did not see, but I believed that he did.

"So what are we going to do?" I asked him.

Bob picked up the blueprint, turned it over, and held it up to the light. "You're going to turn it over," he said. "You're going to flip the whole thing the other way around and learn to love seeing the woods while you're washing dishes."

And that is exactly what we did. We also moved the driveway from the front of the house to the back, added a freestanding garage with a workshop for Ed, and saved a flat place outside the mudroom for my clothesline. The congregation was not alone in seeing this house as a sign that I meant to stay put. I saw it the same way. Beyond that, I saw the house as my bid for a larger life, with more room in it for things that had nothing to do with church. In addition to a clothesline, I wanted a garden, a small orchard, and a fenced pasture for a couple of horses. I wanted a quiet place I could come home to at night and sit on the porch with all the lights off. I wanted a sanctuary, and, though I did not seem able to rope off such a place inside myself, I still held out hope that if I could build one outside myself then perhaps the inner one would grow.

Because Ed and I wanted to be there while our house went up, we went shopping for a house trailer we could park at the bottom of the hill. At Vivian's Mobile Homes we learned to call what we were looking for a "manufactured home," and we furthermore discovered just how many variations on that theme there were. We looked at single-wides and double-wides that came with porches and fireplaces. We looked at manufactured homes with picture windows and hot tubs, dish-washers and home entertainment centers, finally settling on a single-wide with two bedrooms and two baths.

Once we had hauled the trailer to its place in the shade of three poplar trees, I went inside and turned on the kitchen faucet. Nothing came out, which was the beginning of my en-lightenment. Not only were we going to have to dig a well and install a septic tank, we were also going to have to pay Haber-sham Electric Membership Corporation and Standard Tele-phone Company whatever they charged to run wires all the way out to the middle of a former cow pasture. The fact that this had not yet occurred to me confirms everything that country people say about city people who move to the country.

A few days later, a huge red truck appeared with an enor-mous drill bit on it. After clanking his way across some groundhog burrows, the man from Davidson Well Drilling killed the engine, climbed out of the cab, and squinted at the land. I had hoped to meet a real live water witch, but this man was more of a geologist. He guessed where water might be by

the lay of the land, preferring valleys to hills. By the next afternoon I wondered if he should learn to use a dowsing rod instead. He had drilled three large holes in the ground and
struck nothing but rock.

As I watched him position his drill over spot number four, I
began to see him as a lab technician trying to find a vein. The
body of the land lay still beneath his probing. Under its surface
ran rivers of life, which I was trying to tap into. My own life
depended on the transfusion. Without it, I could not drink,
cook, bathe, water plants and animals, or wash clothes. With it,
I could make a home.

When I heard a yell go up, I knew that the fourth "stick" had
worked. The earth had granted me a lifeline, by letting me siphon
off some of the water that was on its way somewhere else. Because of me, there would be less water flowing into the Chattahoochee River: less for the speckled trout, less for the wood
ducks, less for the mountain laurel that drop their white petals
into the river every fall. There would be more water flowing into
my septic tank, laced with laundry detergent, dish soap, and
human waste. At that moment of high awareness, I promised the
land that I would go easy on the water. I would remember where
it came from. I would remain grateful for the sacrifice.

From the day the hole for our basement was dug, I began
living a double life. Our builder was often at our door before
breakfast, asking us whether we wanted wood doors or hollow
core, copper water lines or PVC. Once I had arrived at church
and caught up on telephone calls, I would steal a look at a
lighting catalog before I opened the hymnal to choose the
hymns for Sunday. At lunch I would meet Ed to pick out door-

knobs and pay a hospital call on my way back to church. I had never had a hobby before, but building a house gave me some idea what having one might be like. Every day I looked forward to doing something unrelated to my work, especially if it involved going to the hardware store. I spent so much of my time dealing with words and feelings that I found dealing with sink faucets and switch plates a thrilling change.

We lived in the trailer for nine months, watching the house on the hill grow with every sunset. I learned that the reason there is so much junk stacked outside some house trailers is because there is no room to stack it inside them. When tornado season arrived, I also borrowed the fear of those who live in trailers by necessity and not by choice. In the midst of a five-star thunderstorm, the whole place shook like a boat on the open sea. Scarier still were the late afternoons when the sky turned green and the lifeless air hung over the land like a damp cloth. Ed and I had our own tornado drill: at the first sound of a freight train, we would both grab a cat and head out the nearest window.

For my birthday that year Ed gave me my first outdoors clothesline, where towels and sheets soaked up the September smells of drying hay and turning leaves. We lived on vegetables from the garden, fell asleep to the sound of whip-poor-wills, and drank water from the well until we forgot the taste of chlorine. One day in the spring of 1995, the house was finished. We shook the builder's hand, thanked him for a job well done, and watched his truck disappear down the gravel driveway. That evening I sat down to see the sun set from my new front porch for the first time and wondered what, exactly, I had done right to be right where I was.

Because I had been spending so much time on the house, I worried when certain people began acting strangely at church. When they saw me, they dropped their voices. Some would even end their conversations, giving me a perfunctory wave before they climbed into their cars and drove away. Since a couple of these people served on the church vestry, I began to wonder if I were in big trouble. Maybe they were planning to tell me they were expecting a little more from me now that the date for the housewarming party had been set. Maybe they were going to ask me to sit down with them and reorder my priorities. I hoped that was all it was, but I picked up my tempo at church all the same.

On the Sunday afternoon of the housewarming, people poured onto the front porch of our new home. Bob brought a Japanese maple to plant outside the kitchen window. John brought a basket full of dried hydrangeas to set on the dining room table. While we were admiring these gifts and more, swamped with gratitude for these people, this house, this land, this work, the senior warden called the crowd to order right there on the porch. The congregation had taken up a collection, he said, and they had something to give Ed and me that they hoped would make us feel right at home. Then he looked down the sidewalk, where people I could not see were carrying two beautiful rush-backed rocking chairs our way. When they arrived on the porch, Ed and I tried the rockers out while everybody clapped.

Thank God, I thought. The chairs explained the strange behavior at church. I was not being fired. I was being invited to sit down and stay a while, which I fully intended to do.

Over the next several years, Grace-Calvary Church and I enjoyed our extended honeymoon. The congregation that was plucky enough to call the first woman pastor in Habersham County also had the vision to start a new church in neighboring White County, even though that meant letting a third of our membership go. We hired a second priest to tend the mission while new members arrived to fill the empty seats at Grace-Calvary. We established the first church-related counseling center in the county and opened a hospice office in the parish house.

Grace-Calvary's redheaded organist was fearlessly inventive. She could play Negro spirituals one Sunday and lead the choir in Fauré's *Requiem* the next, getting more sound out of one nineteenth-century keyboard and fifteen volunteer voices than seemed acoustically possible. My first Pentecost Sunday, Miriam agreed to a jazz mass, which seemed like an inspired idea until I walked into the sacristy and found the head of the altar guild setting out the silver. The guest musicians were warming up in the church, and we could both hear a clarinet that sounded as if it had stayed up all night on Bourbon Street.

"Good morning, Helen," I said, but she would not look at me.

"Music like that in church," she said, rubbing hard at the silver.

I should have known not to try something like this so soon, I thought, shifting into Lamaze breathing. If she hates it, then everyone else over fifty is going to hate it too, which includes just about everyone who risked offering me this job. The service starts in eleven minutes. What am I going to do?

"Makes me want to *dance,*" Helen said, lifting her hands above her head and snapping her fingers as she sashayed around the sacristy in her flowered print dress.

When the mission became the Episcopal Church of the Resurrection, I lost my associate, Steve, who became that congregation's full-time rector. Soon the vestry and I decided to hire another full-time staff member to work with youth before we had any idea where the money was coming from. When we found Rob, he was fresh out of seminary, with such gifts for ministry that the money followed. So did enough newcomers to fill every pew. Two Sunday morning services turned into three, as visitors arrived to check out what was going on at Grace-Calvary Church. When I asked one woman with two young daughters why she had come, she said, "You don't scare my kids. I didn't know there was a church like this."

Sundays were the best. I know clergy who say they cannot worship and lead worship at the same time, but I am not one of them. I never liked the panic before the service, when I served as a human memo board for every question and concern that people had to post *somewhere* before they could settle down to pray, but once everyone was seated and the first hymn began, it was foretaste-of-heaven time.

Our bread was given, not earned. We had nowhere else to go and nothing else to do but sit there together, saying sonorous words in unison, listening to language we did not hear anywhere else in our lives. *Take heart. Go in peace. Bear fruit.* Although we could have sat quietly with Bibles on our laps and read these things to ourselves, we took turns reading them out loud to each other instead. The words sounded different when Kline read them than they did when Kathy read them. They sounded different from the mouth of a young mother than they did from the mouth of a widow. This was because the words did not come straight off the page. They percolated up through the silt and gravel of real people's lives so that the meaning in them was fluid, not fixed. Listening to one another read Holy Scripture, some of us learned what is meant by "the living word of God."

We also sang things we could more easily have said. *The Lord be with you. And also with you.* None of us would have dreamed of doing this in the grocery store, but by doing it in church we remembered that there was another way to address one another. *Lift up your hearts. We lift them up unto the Lord.* Where else did any of us sing anymore, especially with other people? Where else could someone pick up the alto line on the second verse of "Amazing Grace" and give five other people the courage to sing in harmony? Sometimes, when we were through, we would all just stand there listening until the last note turned entirely to air.

We could even be quiet together, which was something else that did not happen many other places in our lives. Silence was so countercultural for most of us that it took a lot of practice before we could do it together. At first, when one of us paused after reading a prayer out loud, the rest of us would tense up. *Did she lose her place? Is it someone else's turn to speak? Maybe mine?* But after a while we learned how many ripples one prayer can spread when another does not land right on top of it.

I learned to love hearing the world outside while we were praying for it inside. The sound of an airplane brought all those aboard into church—the fussy babies, the slack-jawed sleepers, the bored businessmen playing games on their laptops. *For those who travel on land, on water, or in the air, let us pray to the Lord.* The sound of an ambulance spoke for the scared person lying on the stretcher inside. *For the aged and infirm, for the widowed and orphans, and for the sick and the suffering, let us pray to the Lord.* The sound of the wind in the pines made music that rivaled anything we were singing inside. *For the good earth which God has given us, and for the wisdom and will to conserve it, let us pray to the Lord.*

Every now and then I would forget to eat breakfast so that the loudest of all these sounds was the gaseous racket of my stomach. This may be the real reason many of us fear silence in church—because anyone sitting near us may hear the hissing, rumbling, wheezing sounds of a living human being, which do not match up with the attractive countenances that we work so hard to present to one another. Since these are the sounds of being human, I even learned to love hearing them while sitting quietly in church. *For real hunger, for twisted guts, and for our inability to conceal them, let us pray to the Lord.*

I like to think that silence was not only one of the best gifts we had to offer our young ones but also one of the signs that the Holy Spirit had come among us. On what turned out to be the noisiest morning of my tenure at Grace-Calvary, I had decided to baptize a whole crowd of babies at the same service. I did this both because I wanted the parents and godparents to know one another and because I wanted the infants to have company. The decision was not popular. Most of the families would have preferred being the only honorees, which is understandable. Most of us like thinking we are God's only children.

By baptizing a crowd, I hoped to give those only children some metaphysical brothers and sisters. Even if they did not remember one thing about the day, maybe they would grow up with a mystical link to one another. Even if they entirely lost track of one another, maybe one day they would gaze at a picture taken of them at their baptisms and wonder who all those other babies had turned out to be. At least one of the purposes of church is to remind us that God has other children, easily as precious as we. Baptism and narcissism cancel each other out.

While my logic may have been good, the logistics were awful. Grace-Calvary is a small church. Divide the square footage by five crying babies, and you get one crying baby per sixteen seats, not counting the anxious parents who only make things worse by trying to make the babies hush. The babies cried through the first hymn, picked up steam through the second, and were going so strong during the reading of the gospel that I decided to ditch my sermon altogether. I folded my manuscript in half and tucked it inside the lectern. I walked to altar rail, where I said something funny about the crying and something straightforward about the baptism. Then I poured the water into the font, led the congregation through the prayers, and called the first family forward to present the first child.

Because remembering is often better than being there, I can no longer say for sure when the howling turned to whimpering and the whimpering to snuffling, but by the time I had the last baby in my arms, the whole place was quiet. The Holy Spirit had spread her wings, and all the babies had settled down underneath them. The child I was about to baptize looked up at me with wet, clear eyes. When I poured water on his head, he beat his fists together and kept looking at me without so much as a hiccup. As the water dripped from his fragrant head back into the font, the ripples of silence spread from there over the heads of the other babies cooing in their parents' arms to the visitors sitting in the last pew. As the silence bounced off the back wall of the church and headed back toward the altar again, a collective sigh went up from close to a hundred people. Some of us still talk about what happened that day.

It was a version of what had happened to me on the river, when I lost track of my small self in the larger scheme of things. There in the church, for close to ten minutes, the babies, the people, the water, and the silence were all one in the spirit. While our individual waves still formed and crested, they also fell back into the same vast deep that both gave rise to us and accepted us back again, to be mixed with one another, washed, and returned. Those who are not afraid of the language call it *mystical union*. "The eye with which I look at God," Meister Eckhart once wrote, "is the same eye with which God looks at me."

Since true bliss is never more than a hair away from sorrow, I learned not to cling to such mornings. The chances were always good that I would be called to the hospital that same afternoon to say a prayer with someone already passing from this world to the next. As much as I hated hospital waiting rooms, I never doubted that I could do some good in them, simply by showing up and staying put. It was one of the times when transference worked in my favor, by letting me into the parts of people's hearts where only God has any right to go. When the old woman who lived in the octagonal house was taken to the emergency room, I sat with one of her three daughters under the fluorescent lights in the waiting room. "I knew Mother would die one day soon," the daughter said when we had read all the battered magazines. "I just didn't think it would be today."

In years to come, when people would ask me what I missed about parish ministry, baptisms and funerals would be high on the list—that, and the children who hung on my legs after the service was over, clinging to my knees while I shook their parents' hands at the door. Because they were not old enough to serve on committees or wrangle over the order of worship, the children often had a better grasp of what church was all about than the rest of us did. When one four-year-old rode by the church with his mother and her out-of-town friend, he interrupted them by tapping at the window. "That," he announced to the friend, "is where God gives us the bread."

Because he was right about that, the congregation grew. God gave us the bread and we gave it to one another. Then we carried it into the community, dishing up soup at the soup

kitchen, handing out food at the food pantry, setting the table
for mothers and their children at the battered women's shelter.
I gained a reputation for preaching. The redheaded organist
was succeeded by another gifted musician. Before long we
were setting out folding chairs at Sunday morning services,
which was when we decided to go from three services to four.
Even with a capable associate who shared leadership of the
liturgy, this meant preaching four times, celebrating communion four times, making announcements four times, and shak-
ing hands four times. It also meant standing from 7:30 in the
morning until after 12:00 noon, so that my old back trouble
returned. When I complained of this to the deacon, he wrote
me a prescription for an orthopedic corset, which became part
of my Sunday vestments. Like Wonder Woman, I acquired a
midsection that was hard as steel.

I was not doing so well on the inside either. In spite of my
best intentions, I had dug myself back into the same hole that
I had left All Saints' to escape. My tiredness was so deep that it
had seeped into my bones. I was out more nights than I was
home. No matter how many new day planners I bought, none
of them told me when I had done enough. If I spent enough
time at the nursing home then I neglected to return telephone
calls, and if I put enough thought into the vestry meeting then
I was less likely to catch mistakes in the Sunday bulletin. As
soon as I managed to convince myself that these were not cardinal sins, one of them would result in an oversight that caused
a parishioner's meltdown.

The demands of parish ministry routinely cut me off from
the resources that enabled me to do parish ministry. I knew

where God's fire was burning, but I could not get to it. I knew how to pray, how to bank the coals and call the Spirit, but by the time I got home each night it was all I could do to pay the bills and go to bed. I pecked God on the cheek the same way I did Ed, drying up inside for want of making love.

More visitors at church meant fewer seats for members. More church services meant that people who went to the early service did not always know people who went to one of the later services. Two strangers who met in an exercise class at Gold's Gym could talk for quite a while before discovering that they were members of the same church. When a beloved member died, there was not always room in the church for all who wanted to attend the funeral, and parish suppers required at least two seatings in order to serve everyone in the parish house.

The obvious solution was to expand our facilities, although I could not imagine adding a capital campaign and a major construction project to our list of things to do. The lay leaders of the parish and I explored the idea for more than a year, holding congregational meetings and hiring consultants to help us clarify our vision, only the vision would not come. While a few members championed the new building, the majority resisted the idea. People were afraid that paying off a new mortgage would decimate our outreach budget. They were afraid that making room for more members would put an end to the intimacy that had drawn them to Grace-Calvary in the first place. Deeper down, they were afraid that leaving the old prayer-soaked church full of memories would break their hearts, rendering them impotent to worship in a new space that stank of paint.

People were afraid, and, even though I thought it was my job to ease their fears, I was afraid too, of all the same things that they were and more. I was afraid that I was not as good at being in charge as I had hoped. I was afraid that I would not be able to manage the conflict that was arising. Above all, I was afraid that I had led the congregation directly into this impasse, which I knew some people blamed openly on me. "We are not going into debt to build you a preaching emporium," one man said during a congregational meeting. When I walked around the parish hall afterward, reading the sheets of newsprint that discussion group leaders had hung on the walls, I saw the same phrase in one form or another on three different sheets: "Wait until Barbara leaves to decide this," they read, which was how I first learned that it was time for me to go.

Like most clergy, I know how to read the signs of depression in others: too many hours in bed, too little affect, too little hope that the deepening darkness will ever lift. According to those who have survived it, depression feels just like it sounds. A great weight descends upon you, pressing you down so that you cannot even lift a hand to help yourself. During the weeks that followed my revelation in the parish hall, I never considered that I might be heading in that direction myself.

For one thing, I was sleeping less instead of more. If a barking dog woke me up in the middle of the night, I would lie there for hours while every demon in the neighborhood came to play on my bed. I imagined being fired. I imagined losing my mind. I imagined discovering that the ache in my back was really a cancer that was eating my bones. After my second cup of tea the next morning, I usually recognized such fears as imaginative ways to be released from my responsibilities without the burden of making a choice.

But if I was low on the sleep scale, then I was high on affect. When I shook people's hands on the porch of the church after services on Sunday, my eyes would start stinging for no reason at all. Had I developed a late-life allergy to boxwood? Had my mascara gone bad? I could not imagine what the problem was, but whatever it was made tears run down my face as I stood there trying to greet people. The children who hugged my knees after services could not see what was going on up above, but their elders could. Every now and then someone would hold out a Kleenex, offering a word of consolation about whatever was weighing so heavily on my heart.

"I'm not crying, really," I would protest, wiping my cheek with my sleeve. "I just got something in my eye." I believed this myself until one Sunday when I climbed in my car after everyone else had gone home. I thought that maybe if I just let my eyes run for a minute instead of mopping them, then whatever was stuck in them would come out. So I stopped fighting the tears, and what was stuck in them really *did* come out. In moments I was sobbing out loud, upended by great waves of grief that caught me entirely off guard.

I belonged to at least three clergy groups at that time, including one in which I could tell the truth, but many of the things that were shifting inside of me seemed too shameful to talk about out loud. Laid low by what was happening at Grace-Calvary, I did not have the energy to put a positive spin on anything. It was as if I were strapped in a chair, watching the film I had worked on for the past five years get stuck in the projector. Unable to move, I watched the lovely frame in front of me melt and burn, opening up a hole through which I saw things I had managed not to see before.

Behind my luminous images of Sunday mornings I saw the committee meetings, the numbing routines, and the chronically difficult people who took up such a large part of my time. Behind my heroic image of myself I saw my tiresome perfectionism, my resentment of those who did not try as hard as I did, and my huge appetite for approval. I saw the forgiving faces of my family, left behind every holiday for the past fifteen years, while I went to conduct services for other people and their families.

Above all, I saw that my desire to draw as near to God as I could had backfired on me somehow. Drawn to care for hurt things, I had ended up with compassion fatigue. Drawn to a life of servanthood, I had ended up a service provider. Drawn to marry the Divine Presence, I had ended up estranged. Like the bluebirds that sat on my windowsills at home, pecking at the reflections they saw in the glass, I could not reach the greenness for which my soul longed. For years I had believed that if I just kept at it, the glass would finally disappear. Now, for the first time, I wondered if I had devoted myself to an illusion.

One quiet afternoon while I was reading at home I heard a loud thump from the front porch, as if someone had pitched a newspaper against the front door. Opening it, I saw the soft bird with the broken neck lying on the floorboards. When I picked her up, her eyes were still clear. Turning around to see what the bird had seen, I looked at the reflection of Mount

Yonah in the window glass, flanked by deep trees and crowned with a great expanse of sky. Poor bird. She had thought all that was ahead of her, had perhaps even chosen the spot she wanted to scout for a nest, when it was really behind her instead, in the direction from which she had come.

# CHAPTER

# 9

B ecause this is a love story, it is difficult to say what went wrong between the Church and me. On the one hand, it was the best of parish ministry that did me in. Grace-Calvary was in trouble because the congregation was growing. I was in trouble because I was doing my job the only way I knew how. On the other hand, there was a definite hardening taking place, not only at Grace-Calvary but at every church I knew. The presenting issue was human sexuality. While the Episcopal Church had gladly received the ministry of gay and lesbian people for as long as anyone could remember, it had done so without blessing the "gay and lesbian" part. The unspoken deal was that the ministry could continue as long as the sexuality stayed under cover. When the Episcopal Church began to question this duplicity at the legislative level, the tremors spread quickly in every direction.

Because Christians are people of the Book, these tremors led quickly to a search of Holy Scripture by partisans on both sides. This, in turn, led to passionate debates about the authority of scripture, the mind of Christ, and the will of God.

At the same time that Grace-Calvary was holding parish meetings about our future, we were also holding meetings about human sexuality mandated by our denomination. This meant that we were discussing whether to build a new church at the same time that we were discussing whether to ordain openly gay and lesbian priests to serve the church, which set up a deep conflict in some people's minds.

Since I had prospered under the care and guidance of inspired priests whom I supposed to be gay, there was no question in my mind about the value of their ministries. But since I was also responsible for the care of souls who did not share my conviction, I learned to feign neutrality as I presided over increasingly bitter debates. If there were anything simple about these debates, they would not still be going on. What I noticed at Grace-Calvary is the same thing I notice whenever people aim to solve their conflicts with one another by turning to the Bible: defending the dried ink marks on the page becomes more vital than defending the neighbor. As a general rule, I would say that human beings never behave more badly toward one another than when they believe they are protecting God. In the words of Arun Gandhi, grandson of Mohandas, "People of the Book risk putting the book above people."

As much as I love the written word, I am aware of the ways this love removes me from the world. The day after the alphabet was invented, someone started thinking up patterns of letters that would stand for real things. S-T-A-R would stand for those bright points of light in the night sky that did not burn the eye as the sun did. L-I-L-Y would stand for the sweet-smelling trumpets that grew in the shade of the biggest trees, and R-I-V-E-R would stand for that broad expanse of wetness that grew to a pounding torrent after R-A-I-N fell from the sky. Eventually, the very sight of these words on a page would evoke their presence through the genius of the human imagination so that it became possible to see a star, smell a lily, or swim in a river without ever making physical contact with any of these things. Better yet, meeting them on the page did not carry the same risks of stinging bees, biting snakes, or chilling currents that meeting them in the flesh did. The words offered detours around all such dangers.

I know that the Bible is a special kind of book, but I find it as seductive as any other. If I am not careful, I can begin to mistake the words on the page for the realities they describe. I can begin to love the dried ink marks on the page more than I love the encounters that gave rise to them. If I am not careful, I can decide that I am really much happier reading my Bible than I am entering into what God is doing in my own time and place, since shutting the book to go outside will involve the very great risk of taking part in stories that are still taking shape. Neither I nor anyone else knows how these stories will turn out, since at this point they involve more blood than ink. The whole purpose of the Bible, it seems to me, is to convince people to set the written word down in order to become living words in the world for God's sake. For me, this willing conversion of ink back to blood is the full substance of faith.

In practice, this means that my faith is far more relational than doctrinal. Although I am guilty of reading scripture as selectively as anyone, my reading persuades me that God is found in right relationships, not in right ideas, and that a great deal of Christian theology began as a stammering response to something that had actually happened in the world. Because Jesus died instead of ushering in the messianic age, Paul responded with a doctrine of atonement. Because the risen Christ struck his followers as very close kin to God, the early church responded with a doctrine of the Trinity. Because Christians did not turn out to be much better behaved than anyone else, Augustine responded with a doctrine of original sin.

The doctrines are works of genius, for the most part, but like books they tend to draw people's attention away from the living human neighbors who are standing right in front of them. They can also lead people to look to outer authorities for direction instead of to the inner teaching of the Holy Spirit. At Grace-Calvary, a parish with both gay and lesbian members, I grew increasingly weary of arguing over what Paul and the author of Leviticus may or may not have meant in half a dozen passages written a couple of thousand years ago while I watched living human beings wince at the vitriol they heard from those with whom they worshiped God.

Human sexuality was only one of the issues dividing Christians in those days. We could also argue about the inspiration of scripture, the uniqueness of Jesus, and the salvation of non-Christians. We could argue about abortion, gun control, just war, and capital punishment. Few of these were live fights at Grace-Calvary, where the congregation had long ago learned to live with its own religious diversity, but the tension in the larger church and culture took its toll on people already alarmed by the rapid changes in their midst.

The things dividing us at Grace-Calvary concerned me less than what the division itself was doing to the community. Because church people tend to think they should not fight, most of them are really bad at it. Many prefer writing long, single-spaced letters to the rector in lieu of direct confrontation. Some sit on their grievances with pained looks on their faces until internal combustion occurs and fire shoots out of their mouths, while others simply vanish, calling the church office months later to remove their names from the rolls. When face-to-face conflict does occur, it is often hard for church people to say what is bothering them in personal terms, especially when what is bothering them cuts close to the bone of what they hold most dear. Many find that they can avoid confessing their sorest fears by speaking of church doctrine instead, or appealing to orthodox Christian belief for support.

Once I had begun crying on a regular basis, I realized just how little interest I had in defending Christian beliefs. The parts of the Christian story that had drawn me into the Church were not the believing parts but the beholding parts.

"Behold, I bring you good tidings of great joy . . ."

"Behold the Lamb of God . . ."

"Behold, I stand at the door and knock . . ."

Whether the narratives starred hayseed shepherds confronted by hosts of glittering angels or desert pilgrims watching something like a dove descend upon a man in a river as a voice from heaven called him "Beloved," Christian faith seemed to depend on beholding things that were clearly beyond belief, including Jesus's own teaching that acts of mercy toward perfect strangers were acts of mercy toward him.

While I understood both why and how the early church had decided to wrap those mysteries in protective layers of orthodox belief, the beliefs never seized my heart the way the mysteries did.

I did not think I was alone in this. Both at All Saints' and at Grace-Calvary, I had spent hours talking with people who had trouble believing. For some, the issue was that they believed *less* than they thought they should about Jesus. They were not troubled by the idea that he may have had two human parents instead of one or that his real presence with his disciples after his death might have been more metaphysical than physical. The glory they beheld in him had more to do with the nature of his being than with the number of his miracles, but they had suffered enough at the hands of true believers to learn to keep their mouths shut.

For others, the issue was that they believed *more* than Jesus. Having beheld his glory, they found themselves running into God's glory all over the place, including places where Christian doctrine said that it should not be. I knew Christians who had beheld God's glory in a Lakota sweat lodge, in a sacred Celtic grove, and at the edge of a Hawaiian volcano, as well as in dreams and visions that they were afraid to tell anyone else about at all. These people not only feared being shunned for their unorthodox narratives, they also feared sharing some of the most powerful things that had ever happened to them with people who might dismiss them.

Given the history of Christians as a people who started out beholding what was beyond belief, this struck me as a lamentable state of affairs, both for those who have learned to see no more than they are supposed to see as well as for those who have excused themselves from traditional churches because they see too little or too much. If it is true that God exceeds all our efforts to contain God, then is it too big a stretch to declare that *dumbfoundedness* is what all Christians have most in common? Or that coming together to confess all that we do not know is at least as sacred an activity as declaring what we think we do know?

I had become an Episcopalian in the first place because the Anglican way cared more for common prayer than for right belief, but under stress even Episcopalians began vetting one another on the virgin birth, the divinity of Jesus, and his physical resurrection from the dead. Both in Clarkesville and elsewhere, the poets began drifting away from churches as the jurists grew louder and more insistent. I began to feel like a defense attorney for those who could not square their love of God and neighbor with the terms of the Nicene Creed, while my flagging attempt to be all things to all people was turning into a bad case of amnesia about my own Christian identity. My role and my soul were eating each other alive. I wanted out of the belief business and back into the beholding business. I wanted to recover the kind of faith that has nothing to do with being sure what I believe and everything to do with trusting God to catch me though I am not sure of anything.

Because I did not know how to give my soul what it wanted, I continued to play my role, becoming more brittle with every passing day. I moved papers around on my desk without focusing on any of them. I quit answering the telephone on my days off. Some Fridays I would stand in the kitchen looking at the blinking red light on the answering machine without ever finding the strength to reach out my hand and press Play. What if someone had died? What if someone really needed help? Because I had become that someone, I could not answer the telephone. Whoever was on the other end would have to call the next person on the list.

Even Sundays began to shut down on me. When the baptismal covenant was part of the service, I could feel myself stiffen as I approached the fourth question.

"Will you seek and serve Christ in all persons," I asked the congregation, "loving your neighbor as yourself?"

In unison they read the answer printed in the Book of Common Prayer.

"I will, with God's help," they responded faithfully, while I stifled my protest. *All persons?* How could I possibly seek and serve Christ in *all persons?* Did the author of that response have any idea how many hungry, needy, angry, manipulative, deeply ill people I saw in the course of a week? I knew that I could treat most of them with courtesy and care. I could offer the rest a fair hearing. I could even take a stab at mediating God's love to them, but the idea of opening myself to every one of them as I opened myself to Christ had become out of the question.

Like Grandfather Abraham, I tried to bargain God down. *I can do twenty, maybe thirty,* I offered. *Will you accept twenty-five?* Along with the difficult people there were people whose feet I would have gladly washed if I could have gotten them to take their socks off. Unlike the difficult ones, these people did not ask for much from me. They tended to be givers, not takers, and if they asked for help then I knew that their resources were truly exhausted. I am not sure that I served Christ in them as much as I met Christ in them, but either way they were not the problem. The problem was that I wanted everyone to be like them.

Having tried as hard as I knew how to seek and serve Christ in all persons, I knew for sure that I could not do it. I was not even sure that I wanted to do it anymore, and I felt increasingly deceitful saying that I would. Feeding people was no longer feeding me. While I remained constitutionally incapable of walking past a hungry baby bird, it was the wild geese that were calling to me. When I heard them coming, I hurried to the window, straining to see them through the branches of the tall pines overhead. Sometimes all I caught was a beating wing or an outstretched neck, but even that was enough to set me weeping again. No thoughts went with the tears. The tears simply fell out of my eyes, and it was not until the geese were gone that the words formed in the empty air. *Take me with you.*

But how could I leave? I had committed myself to the care of Grace-Calvary Church. I had accepted both holy orders and rocking chairs. I had pledged my troth. Plus, my young associate, Rob, and his wife, Sara, had just bought a house. She was pregnant with their first child. They had moved to Clarkesville on the promise of at least two years at Grace-Calvary. If I left they would have to leave too.

And where would I go? Anyone who has ever contemplated divorce knows that at some point you have to ask the question, "Is the problem with me and this partner, or is the problem with me and the institution of marriage?" There was no sense seeking a position at another church if my problem was with the institution, and, besides, I did not want to move. How and where I lived had become more important to me than what I did for a living. I could not imagine watching the sun set over any other tree line or doing without the sound of the peepers in the spring. I could not imagine giving away the chickens or finding homes for the horses. Above all, I could not imagine abandoning the land.

So I began to do what every full-time parish minister should probably do on a regular basis, or at least those who worry about losing their jobs more than they worry about losing their souls. I began thinking about what else I could do for a living. I could apply for a job at The Book Cellar on the square. I could cook for a small restaurant. I could talk Ed into buying a hardware store and learn how to operate the cash register. Since ordained ministry generally involves three years of graduate study and counts as one of "the professions," the alternatives I came up with all involved significant loss of status. I remembered one priest I knew whose ill health had led her to resign from her church to take a part-time position at a bookstore. I also remembered how sorry I felt for her when I saw her there, not because she was sick but because I thought she had taken such a big step down. I had been wearing my collar for about six months by then, and I wore it like a string of thousand-dollar pearls. Fifteen years later, I was ready to hang it up.

One gooseless afternoon I was sitting in my office sorting mail when the telephone rang. I was expecting a call from home so I answered it, but the call was not from home. It was from Piedmont College, a small four-year liberal arts college just down the road, where more than a dozen members of Grace-Calvary worked or taught. I had been in clergy groups with chaplains of the college and had borrowed books from the library, but none of that explained why the president of the college was calling me.

He wanted to tell me about a new position that was opening up, he said. The board of trustees had decided to establish a new major in religion and philosophy. Congregational churches across the country had raised money to endow a new chair. Would I consider becoming a candidate?

His question was so unexpected that it erased my memory tapes. I do not remember what I said, except that it must have sounded like no, because when I had finished talking the president said, "Well, I hope you'll think about it." I did think about it. I thought about it so much that the next day I called him back and said, "Would you say what you said yesterday one more time?" He did, and this time I said, "Yes, please, yes, consider me a candidate."

While the college conducted a formal search, I spoke with my bishop, who was not surprised by my decision. Then I spoke with Rob, whose job would be placed in jeopardy by my leaving. My conversation with him was the hardest one, as well as the one in which I was prepared to accept the most blame. When this young priest received my news with grace instead of anger, he reminded me that salvation is not something that happens only at the end of a person's life. Salvation happens every time someone with a key uses it to open a door he could lock instead.

When the president called back to offer me the job, I took it. The next day I began making telephone calls. Beginning with the nine members of the vestry, I worked my way down the parish directory, calling everyone whom I wanted to hear the news from me instead of from someone else. Some were shocked and some were saddened, while others sounded plainly relieved. "If that's what you want, then go for it," said the captain of the church softball team, while someone else accused me of breaking my word.

"You said you would stay ten years," she reminded me. "I know," I said. "I really believed it too."

After I had finished the calls I composed a letter to send to everyone on the parish mailing list. After that I sat and stared at my office. In church circles, the word means not only the room where a pastor keeps a desk, a chair, and enough books to look educated but also the position of trust that he or she holds. While a visitor might have noted the Bibles and prayer books on my desk or the ordination certificate hanging on the wall as evidence of that trust, I knew that the real signs were in the bathroom.

That was where I kept the things people had given me over the years, in the old linen closet with a single lightbulb overhead. I pulled the string and the light came on, illuminating the red Saint Barbara candle someone had found in the international food section at the grocery store, the giant sand dollar someone else had brought back from vacation, and the child's papier-mâché sculpture of me in a clerical collar riding a brown horse.

Behind that stood a forest of old flower vases, a black plastic box that had once held the ashes of someone with no family left, and a small needlepoint that read "Jesus" if you could discern the letters in the geometrical design. There was a pastel drawing on black construction paper of one candle burning in a window, made for me by a young man in a psychiatric hospital, and underneath that, some pen-and-ink sketches of churches given to me by a retired priest. What was I to do with these things, especially since it was not the things themselves but the act of receiving them that had mattered?

Next to the linen closet stood a storage cabinet installed over the old pink bathtub, which held everything from Grace-Calvary stationery to answer blanks for the Myers-Briggs Type Indicator. Most of that could stay, I decided, but the four-drawer file cabinet was going to need some careful weeding. Sitting down on the lid of the pink toilet, I began to go through the folders. There were close to two hundred of them in the first two drawers, where I kept resources for every Sunday in the three-year lectionary cycle. Crowded in the third drawer were folders for every one of Grace-Calvary's many parish groups and committees. Children's Chapel. Confirmation Class. Journey to Adulthood. Daughters of the King. Stewardship. Annual Budget. Parochial Report. Buildings and Grounds. A/V Equipment. Northeast Georgia Convocation. Clarkesville Ministers' Association. The bottom drawer held everything that would not fit anywhere else. Years of church correspondence were there, along with fat folders full of ideas for Christian education classes, parish retreats, and Wednesday night suppers.

The folders went on and on, convicting me by their sheer numbers of the sin of omnicompetence. Who could be good at so many different things? What had driven me to try? According to a vocational test I once took, I would have made an excellent accountant or research librarian, both specialized vocations that might have allowed me to focus on doing one thing well. Instead I became a generalist, with a whole file cabinet full of things that would never get done no matter how many hours I spent on them.

Abandoning them at last gave me a great sense of relief. I kept New Hymns, Blessing of Animals, and the sermons. I also took a few note cards with Julian of Norwich's famous benediction on them. *And all shall be well, and all shall be well, and all manner of thing shall be well.* Then I slid the bottom drawer shut and heard it click for the last time.

During these last weeks at church, I received an invitation from a couple of church members to attend an annual pool party at their home. The party was legendary, involving live Maine lobsters and kegs of imported beer. I did not remember ever having been invited before, perhaps because everyone knew I spent Saturday nights at home, but this time I was eager to go.

When I arrived, the veranda of the old Victorian cottage was packed with people, only the nearest of whom greeted me as I climbed the wide wooden steps. Instead of working the crowd, I accepted a cold cup of beer from the keg and sat down on the porch swing to talk with a layman whom I knew well. We did not talk church business, for once, and since I no longer had any power to wield for good or for ill, our conversation was missing the usual deference and discretion. We talked about how his garden was doing and what I was going to do with my couple of months off. Why hadn't I realized before how likable he was?

After I left him in search of food, I wound up with a couple I had always thought I would enjoy but whom I never really got to know since they did not serve on any committees and were never, as far as I knew, in crisis. We sat down in adjacent rocking chairs with plates full of lobster and corn balanced on our laps, laughing so much that I spit food clear across the porch. I did not wonder why I had not sought them out earlier because I already knew the answer. By my rules, caring for troubled people always took precedence over enjoying delightful people, and the line of troubled people never ended. Sitting there with corn stuck between my teeth, I wondered why I had not changed that rule sooner.

After my supper had settled I wandered down to the pool, where I watched swimming children splitting beams of underwater light with their bodies. I had baptized many of them, and I loved seeing them all shrieking and paddling around together in that one big pool. Suddenly to my right there was a deeper yell, the sound of scrabbling feet on cement, and then a large plop as a fully clothed adult landed in the water.

I stood back and watched the mayhem that ensued. All around me, people were grabbing people and wrestling them toward the water. The dark night air was full of pool spray and laughter. The kids were going crazy. Several people hunting for potential victims turned toward me, their faces lit with smiles. When they saw who I was they turned away again so that I felt sad instead of glad. Whatever changes were occurring inside of me, I still looked waterproof to them. Like the sick man in

John's gospel, who lay by the healing pool of Beth-zatha for thirty-eight years because he had no one to put him in when the water was stirred up, I watched others plunging in ahead of me. Then two strong hands grabbed my upper arms from behind, and before I knew it I was in the water, fully immersed and swimming in light.

I never found out who my savior was, but when I broke the surface, I looked around at all of those shining people with makeup running down their cheeks, with hair plastered to their heads, and I was so happy to be one of them. If being ordained meant being set apart from them, then I did not want to be ordained anymore. I wanted to be human. I wanted to spit food and let snot run down my chin. I wanted to confess being as lost and found as anyone else without caring that my underwear showed through my wet clothes. Bobbing in that healing pool with all those other flawed beings of light, I looked around and saw them as I had never seen them before, while some of them looked at me the same way. The long wait had come to an end. I was in the water at last.

lthough I have never found a proper way to use it, I keep a small wooden box full of index cards on the table next to my writing chair. On each card I have recorded some startling fact or pungent quotation that I mean to do more with some day. One reminds me that people who live on ventilators rank their happiness at 5.1 on a scale of 7 while people who breathe on their own score only four-tenths of a point higher for an average of 5.5. "Happiness is reality divided by expectations," says Dr. John Bach, respiratory expert at the University Hospital in Newark, New Jersey.

Sometimes, when I am lost for words, I sort through the cards and pull out those that speak to me. While the possible combinations approach infinity, there are days when some of the cards practically stick to my fingers. "God is not found in the soul by adding anything but by subtracting," reads one by Meister Eckhart. Next to that one goes another by Thérèse of Lisieux. "If you are willing serenely to bear the trial of being displeasing to yourself, then you will be for Jesus a pleasant place of shelter."

A Wallace Stevens card rounds out this small hand. "Perhaps the truth depends on a walk around the lake," the poet says.

As I prepared to leave Grace-Calvary Church, these cards had my fingerprints all over them, but there was one card I did not have to look up because I knew the words on it by heart. The quotation came from Walter Brueggemann, prolific scholar of the Hebrew Bible. "The world for which you have been so carefully prepared is being taken away from you," he said, "by the grace of God."

To get the full punch of that prophecy, I had to pause for breath at least twice along the way. The first pause came as I acknowledged how carefully I had been prepared for priesthood. Counting my four years as a religion major, I had seven years of higher education behind me, plus twenty-one more of working in churches, hospitals, and seminaries. I had completed a full year of Clinical Pastoral Education. I had passed my weeklong General Ordination Exams. I had invested four years in the Clergy Leadership Project and served a couple more on the Commission on Ministry. While there was always more to learn, I had no doubt that I had been carefully prepared. To pause there was to breathe the crisp air of accomplishment.

To keep going was to acknowledge something else that I knew was true. While my friends were becoming bishops and deans of cathedrals, I was falling off the ladder of success. The fact that I had willingly let go of the rungs did nothing to diminish my sense of failure. By leaving church, I was about to leave everything I knew how to do and be. I had no way of knowing whether my choice would turn out to be a good one, and by the time I discovered the answer there would be no going back. To pause there was to feel weightless, with my head on fire while I tried to draw breath.

To finish the sentence was to abandon everything I knew for something I could only trust: that God was in this loss, which was not robbery but relinquishment. I had found the perfect parish in the foothills of north Georgia, where there was no excuse for my not becoming the perfect rector of it. I had built a reputation for preaching and writing, both at the local level and beyond. I had done everything I knew how to do to draw as near to the heart of God as I could, only to find myself out of gas on a lonely road, filled with bitterness and self-pity. To suppose that I had ended up in such a place by the grace of God required a significant leap of faith. If I could open my hands, then all that fell from them might flower on the way down. If I could let myself fall, then I too might land in a fertile place.

Once I had decided to leave Grace-Calvary, I left in a hurry. It would take me years to understand all the reasons why, but at the time all I knew was that I had to get out fast. I felt the same urgency I had felt one morning when I leaned too close to the gas stove in my terrycloth bathrobe. Before I knew it, a blue flame from the burner had leaped to the loose cotton weave on my cuff. While the cloth itself did not catch fire, all the tallest loops did, so that a blaze as fast as a grass fire spread up my right arm, across my shoulders, and down my left arm before I fully registered what was happening. By the time the sparks reached the other cuff, my robe was lying on the kitchen floor, with a thin wisp of smoke twirling up toward the ceiling. I do not recall ever deciding to take it off, but I do recall marveling at my instinct for survival.

Because I did not stay at Grace-Calvary long enough for me or anyone else to resolve my departure at a feeling level, most of the ambivalence about my resignation was funneled into my going-away party. It was a hasty affair, held in the parish hall on a weeknight near the end of September. Enough people came to save me from embarrassment. After some kind words by those with whom I had shared leadership, I was presented with a ceramic soup tureen in the shape of a giant orange pumpkin. Since Thanksgiving was just around the corner, I took that to be what the gift symbolized: gratitude for the five and a half years that I had spent at Grace-Calvary. But the Cinderella in me detected another message that seemed more to the point. Wherever that congregation and I had been going together, our royal carriage had turned back into a pumpkin. The clock had struck midnight, and it was time for me to go.

Or was that just my exit strategy? Looking around the parish hall that night, I was struck hard by all that I was leaving behind. In that one room, I had welcomed dozens of new members, introducing them to the intricacies of Anglican history and theology. I had said prayers at the wakes of those who had died, sung Christmas carols around the old upright piano that needed tuning, and eaten pounds of chicken casseroles at covered dish suppers. Suzanne was there that night, back from her Peace Corps placement in North Africa with a lovely silver bracelet on her arm. The women in her village had given it to her, she said when I admired it. Bing and Maggie were there, smelling faintly of the Chihuahuas who were the children of their old age. Bob and John were there, who had helped site my house before the foundation was dug, and Eleanor, who volunteered early on to be my "other mother" whenever I needed one.

There were so many people in that room whom I had committed to love over the past five and a half years. I might see them again at the grocery store or the post office, but when that happened we would both register the fact that I was no longer their pastor. Standing there with my pumpkin, I forgot why leaving church had ever seemed a welcome prospect to me. I kept the doors of my heart cracked open as speeches were made and more gifts were presented. Then, at the point in the ceremony when the departing rector is supposed to give the keys to the church back to the senior warden, I handed Jerrell the wooden doorstop that had been presented to me when I arrived at Grace-Calvary. "Keep the doors of this church open to all people," read the little brass plaque on the flat end of the wedge. Once I saw it safely in Jerrell's hand, there was nothing to hold the doors of my heart open any longer. They swung shut with a click, so that I was able to say good-bye without weeping to everyone who stood in line.

When they had all gone, I gathered up my things. In addition to the pumpkin, there was a Piedmont College T-shirt, a handful of cards, and a white paper towel with something hard inside. When I picked it up, Suzanne's silver bracelet fell into my hand. I slipped the bright bangle over the worn cuff of my clergy shirt, where I never wore anything more daring than a

Timex watch. Then I turned off the light and stepped into the night. As I did, I heard the familiar honking over my head. Through the pines I could not see the wild geese any better than they could see me, but I took their presence as a blessing. I too was on the move without a map. I too was traveling on pure instinct. Standing there with my face turned up, I felt a string plucked inside of me, thrilling in its tenor. *Take me with you.* Listening to the goose voices disappearing in the dark, I sensed that God did not judge my strong urge to fly.

Late that week, a maintenance crew from Piedmont showed up with a flatbed trailer to transport my things to my new office. In no time at all they had piled my old couch, my chairs, my butler's table, and my oak desk on the trailer, tucking dozens of book boxes in between. Since the trailer was an open one, the driver took his time traveling the six miles between the church and the college, while I followed behind him in case something fell off.

The last time I had driven twenty-five miles per hour down the highway, I had been following a hearse. My headlights were not on this time and no one pulled off on the shoulder of the road as I passed by, but there was still mourning going on in my front seat. I had thought I would stay at Grace-Calvary for ten years at least. I had thought I would be a good rector. I had thought I would know how to lead a congregation, and when I could not see the way ahead I had thought God would give me a vision. Instead, I had resigned with a mortgaged heart and a sense of defeat so great that I had no ready answer for friends who asked me why I left. The easiest thing was to tell them that I had always wanted to teach college, which was true, but behind that answer lay truths harder to confess. My quest to serve God in the church had exhausted my spiritual savings. My dedication to being good had cost me a fortune in being whole. My desire to do all things well had kept me from doing the one thing within my power to do, which was to discover what it meant to be fully human.

My possessions flapped pitifully in the breeze. The last time I had seen them heaped up like that was on the lawn of the parish house after my triumphal entry into Clarkesville. While I wanted this move almost as badly as I had wanted that one, there would be no one waiting for me on the other end this time. I would not meet my first classes until the beginning of the spring semester, which was still three months away. There would be no celebration of new ministry this time, no welcome gifts set in front of my door. Instead, the same crew that had loaded my things would unload them again, packing them into the tiny office in the business school, which was the only one available. Then they would go away and I would be alone, just as I had wanted to be.

By the time the procession reached the college, I had thrown dirt on the coffin and was ready to move furniture. Since only about half of what I owned would fit into my new quarters, I made two piles: things to keep and things to let go. I kept the desk, two chairs, and my grandmother's crystal flower vase. I let go of the couch, the butler's table, and the print of the Reverend Robert Walker ice-skating on Duddingston Loch.

As I passed through the door of my new office with my second load in my arms, I noted the nameplate, which carried no titles or honorifics. "Barbara Taylor," it read, "Religion." The

Master of Divinity had become a member of the Department of Humanities. Feeling both the lightness and the bareness of that description, I hung my father's academic gown on the back of the door, the one black robe that would replace my linen albs and brocade chasubles, my rainbow-colored stoles, my black cassock, surplice, cincture band, and tippet. My divestment had begun.

PART TWO

# Losing

*Vocation puts an end to you in order to disclose your true end.*
RICHARD LISCHER

What do you do the day *after* you change your life? I left Grace-Calvary so quickly that I had spent the last weeks tying up every loose end I could. Like a prisoner who wanted to leave her cell neat after her jail-break, I was so focused on finessing my escape that I did not spare a thought for what I would do the next morning. Then the next morning arrived and I stood looking at a vast salt plain without the first idea what to do next. I was unemployed. There was nowhere I had to be and no one waiting for me to show up. I had a whole Monday on my hands, soon to be followed by a whole Tuesday, a whole Wednesday, and eventually, a whole Sunday to decide what to do with.

The house was as silent as a desert. The hands on the clock were stuck at 9:45 AM, which was when I normally left for church. There were certainly closets to clean and course plans to prepare. I had three substantial speeches to give later in the fall, which still needed plenty of work, and a stack of unanswered correspondence that stretched back at least three months. I had plenty to do, in other words, but that was not unusual. What was unusual was that for once I had plenty of time to do it all, with no one but myself to blame if I did not.

I recognized the feathery panic I felt from a winter long ago, when I was an aspiring short story writer who typed other people's letters for a living. When I was twenty-seven, I saved up a whole year's vacation time from my secretarial job in hopes of being accepted at Yaddo, a writer's colony in upstate New York where John Cheever, Flannery O'Connor, and Sylvia Plath had all lived for short periods of time. If I were granted a winter residency, I would have the whole month of December to do nothing but eat, sleep, and write. There would be no telephone in my room. All of my meals would be prepared for me. Socializing with other residents was forbidden until cocktail hour each day. The rest of the time I was expected to write.

When the acceptance letter arrived, I prepared to enter paradise. I bought and delivered all my Christmas presents ahead of time, paid my bills, packed my most comfortable clothes, and headed north to Saratoga Springs, where snow was already hanging heavy on the hemlocks. When I looked out the leaded glass windows of my charming bedroom, green and white were all I saw. Quiet was all I heard. I arranged my desk with all the faith of a priest setting an altar. The next morning I sat down at it and prepared to receive the inspiration that had been waiting to pour forth.

Instead, I stared at a blank sheet of typing paper until lunch, which gave me such a headache that I lay on my bed the rest of the afternoon with a damp cloth over my eyes. The next day I managed to outline a story, which did not seem worth writing the day after that. The trash can filled up with wadded paper while my first week of paradise ran through my fingers. Soon I was waking up with headaches, which persisted until the night I lay on the floor of my room and confessed the truth to the white ceiling. The pain really was inside my own head. Nothing outside of me had ever prevented me from writing. All of the distractions I had blamed for my lack of traction back home were no more than handy excuses for my own distracted heart. If I wanted things to change, then the place to start was from the inside out and not the other way around.

The week after I left church, I was back on the floor again. For years I had kept hoping that intimacy with God would blossom as soon as I got everything done, got everyone settled, got my environment just right and my calendar cleared. I counted on it to come as a reward for how hard I had worked, or at least as the built-in consequence of a life of service, but even when I managed to meet all of my conditions for a day or two, I was so exhausted from the effort that I could not keep my eyes open. Slumber spirituality took over, and when I woke up I was right back where I started, with miles to go toward the home I never quite reached.

Soon after I moved to the country, a friend from the city set out to see me and got seriously lost. These were the days before cell phones, so she was on her own with nothing but my directions and a badly out-of-date map. Already an hour later than she wanted to be, she was speeding through the little town of Mount Airy when she saw the blue lights in her rearview mirror. I forgot to warn her that Mount Airy was a speed trap. Busted, she pulled over on the shoulder of the road and had her license ready when the officer arrived at her window.

"I am so sorry," she said, handing it to him along with her registration. "I know I was speeding, but I've been lost for the last forty minutes and I cannot find Tower Terrace anywhere on this map."

"Well, I'm sorry about that too, ma'am," he said, writing up her citation, "but what made you think that hurrying would help you find your way?"

What made any of us think that the place we are trying to reach is far, far ahead of us somewhere and that the only way to get there is to run until we drop? For Christians, at least part of the answer is that many of us have been taught to think of God's kingdom as something outside ourselves, for which we must search as a merchant searches for the pearl of great price. But even that points to a larger and more enduring human problem, which is the problem of mortality. With a limited number of years to do whatever it is that we are supposed to be doing here, who has time to stop?

According to the Hebrew Bible, everyone does, for at least one full day every week.

> Remember the Sabbath day, and keep it holy. Six days you shall labor and do all your work. But the seventh day is a Sabbath to the LORD your God; you shall not do any work—you, your son or your daughter, your male or female slave, your livestock, or the alien resident in your towns. For in six days the LORD made heaven and earth,

the sea, and all that is in them, but rested the seventh day;
therefore the LORD blessed the Sabbath day and conse-
crated it. (Exodus 20:8 – 11)

How long had it been since I had remembered the Sabbath?
I was certainly aware of the concept. I had even declared Friday my Sabbath instead of my day off, but on that day, as on
every other day of the week, I stayed very busy. I worked on
my sermon, shifting loads of laundry from the washer to the
clothesline during my frequent breaks, and when that was
done I cleaned the litter boxes, fed the animals, and thought
about what to cook for supper unless I had a wedding re-
hearsal to attend. The only material difference between Friday
and any other day of the week was that I worked at home in
sweat clothes instead of at church in clericals.

Like every other clergyperson I knew, I believed I had no alternative. Taking a full day off was so inconceivable that I made
up reasons why it was not possible. If I stopped for a whole day,
there would be no more weekend weddings at Grace-Calvary, or
someone else would have to do them. Sick people would languish
in the hospital and begin to question their faith. Parishioners
would start a rumor that I was not a real shepherd but only a
hired hand. If I stopped for a whole day, my animals would starve,
my house would grow mold, weeds would take over my garden,
and my credit rating would collapse. If I stopped for a whole day,
God would be sorely disappointed in me.

While remembering the Sabbath really does involve a radi-
cal shift of priorities, these were all lies. Observant Jews have
kept the Sabbath holy for millennia, even those caring for half

a dozen children and elderly parents whose needs do not stop when the sun goes down. Sabbath is written into the ancient covenant with God. Remember the Sabbath, the rabbis say, and you fulfill all of Torah. Stop for one whole day every week, and you will remember what it means to be created in the image of God, who rested on the seventh day not from weariness but from complete freedom. The clear promise is that those who rest like God find themselves free like God, no longer slaves to the thousand compulsions that send others rushing toward their graves.

When I was a junior in high school, my boyfriend Herb played on the varsity basketball team. He was not the star player, however. The star player was a boy named David, who scored so many points during his four-year career that the coach retired his jersey when he graduated. This would have been remarkable under any circumstances, but it was doubly so since David did not play on Friday nights. On Friday nights, David observed the Sabbath with the rest of his family, who generously withdrew when David's gentile friends arrived, sweaty and defeated, after Friday night home games.

David would sit there in his *kippah,* openly delighted with the blow-by-blow description of the game. While the Shabbat candles still flickered on the supper table, every light in the room was on a timer. When one of them clicked off (signaling bedtime), all David had to do was nod and one of us would turn it back on again. We were David's *Shabbat goyim*—his gentile friends who could do things for him on the Sabbath that he could not do for himself—which sometimes included making popcorn in the kosher kitchen.

I still remember the night someone asked David if it did not kill him to have to sit home on Friday nights while his team was getting slaughtered in the high school gymnasium.

"No one *makes* me do this," he said. "I'm a Jew, and Jews observe the Sabbath." Six days a week, he said, he loved nothing more than playing basketball and he gladly gave all he had to the game. On the seventh day, he loved being a Jew more than he loved playing basketball, and he just as gladly gave all he had to the Sabbath. Sure, he felt a tug, but that was the whole point. Sabbath was his chance to remember what was really real. Once three stars were visible in the Friday night sky, his identity as a Jew was more real to him than his identity as the star of our basketball team.

When I was seventeen years old, I had never heard anyone my age say anything like that before. Thirty-seven years later, I remember that living room as clearly as if I were looking at a photograph of it, with David sitting on the sofa like a rabbi teaching the rest of us the way of life. Sabbath was not a burden for him, any more than it was a private day off that he could take or leave. Sabbath was *who he was.* It was his stake in the ongoing life of his community, the one set day each week when he entered into communion with God and his neighbor. As much as I loved the Druid Hills Red Devils, even I could see that there was no contest.

If my first loss upon leaving church was my regular Sunday job, then my first gain was the Sabbath. I resolved that I would worship but I would not work—at anything—for one whole day a week. I would read for pleasure and I would prepare simple food, but any activity prefaced by *ought, should,* or *must* in my mind was automatically disqualified. I would not turn on the computer. I would not pay bills. I would not go near a laundry basket or a litter box.

On that first Sunday, even the prospect of public worship was too much for me. I could not go back to Grace-Calvary, and I could not fathom going anywhere else. I felt like a religious invalid, still weak from my recent fever and embarrassed by how I looked. I did not want to be touched. I did not want to be asked how I was feeling. I did not want to endure any real or imagined questions about what I was doing sitting in a pew instead of standing up front where I belonged. Once the sound of Ed's car had disappeared in the distance, I took a prayer book out on the front porch and read the morning office with the birds.

No one complained about the hymns. I did not sweat the sermon. The best part was the silence—mountains and mountains of it between the populated valleys of the words—with no reason to hurry for fear of holding anyone else up. When I came to Canticle 12, the words flew off the page.

*Let the earth glorify the Lord,*
*praise him and highly exalt him forever.*
*Glorify the Lord, O mountains and hills,*
*and all that grows upon the earth,*
*praise him and highly exalt him forever.*

The view in front of me was half earth and half sky. The stone outcropping on Mount Yonah shone gray through the still green trees. In the pasture, heavy-headed thistles and joe-pye weed both flowered purple while the fallen muscadines fermented on the ground.

> *Glorify the Lord, O springs of water, seas and streams,*
> *O whales and all that move in the waters.*
> *All birds of the air, glorify the Lord,*
> *praise him and highly exalt him forever.*

I heard my neighbor's roosters crowing down the hill. I heard the Chattahoochee River rushing beyond the tree line. There are no whales in it, but I have seen large silver carp sleeping in the shallows while wood ducks skim the surface with their wings.

> *Glorify the Lord, O beasts of the wild,*
> *and all you flocks and herds.*
> *O men and women everywhere, glorify the Lord,*
> *praise him and highly exalt him forever.*

Sitting there on my porch that first Sabbath morning, I understood what Native Americans mean when they speak of "medicine." In the strictest sense, they are speaking of how a little yellow root can help with indigestion or a tea brewed with chamomile can help you sleep. In the broadest sense, they are speaking of the curative power of creation. Sitting there in the healing presence of the mountains, the waters, the birds, and the beasts, I could not recall why I had so often neglected this medicine, though it was lying all around me. What had led me to choose aspirin over purple flowers or Tums over wood ducks? Was it because I could chew them on the go, without having to sit down so they could minister to me? Or was it because I feared what might bubble up if I sat down?

Anyone who practices Sabbath for even an afternoon usually suffers a little spell of Sabbath sickness. Once you have finished the paper and the second pot of tea, you can start feeling a little jumpy, a little ready to get back to work. You can discover the true meaning of *rationalization,* which is what your mind does when it wants to do something that you have decided you will not do. Is yard work really work if you enjoy it? Is flipping through a mail-order catalog really shopping? *Yes, it is.*

If you decide to live on the fire that God has kindled inside of you instead of rushing out to find some sticks to rub together, then it does not take long for all sorts of feelings to come out of hiding. You can find yourself crying buckets of uncried tears over things you thought you had handled years ago. People you have loved and lost can show up with their ghostly lawn chairs, announcing they have nowhere else they have to be all day. While you are talking with them, you may gradually become aware of an aching leg and look down to see a bruise on your thigh that you did not know you had. How many other collisions did you ignore in your rush from here to there?

That first Sunday, I had time to press all kinds of bruises, both real and imagined, but for once I did not crash into anything that made a new one. I also discovered the freedom of the Sabbath. Released from bondage to the clock, I ate when I was hungry instead of when I had to. I found out that I was far less hungry for groceries than for the bread I could not buy. When I slowed down, I could feel my pulse beating under my chin, like a small bird nestled against my neck. The girdle of my diaphragm loosened, causing great sighs too deep for words to pour from my body. In their wake, I discovered more room around my heart, a greater capacity for fresh air.

Sabbath sickness turned out to be a lot like other sicknesses, which until then had been the only way I could justify more than one night's rest. I had never been any good at saying no. *No, I won't. No, not today.* Phrases like these struck me as the antithesis of the gospel. When did Jesus ever say no to anyone who needed something from him? To follow his example meant skipping meals in order to tend the people lined up at the door. It meant abandoning your plans to get away and rest for a while when you saw how many people had followed you to your resting place. It meant giving to everyone who begged from you, going the extra mile, and handing your cloak to someone who had only asked you for your shirt. Didn't Jesus get in trouble for doing things on the Sabbath that he was not supposed to do?

I decided to take a rest from trying to be Jesus too. *No, I won't. No, not today.* Today I will consent to be an extra in God's drama, someone off to the side watching the scenery unfold with self-forgetfulness that is not available to me at center stage. Today I will bear the narcissistic wound of knowing that there are others who can say my lines when I am not there, including some who can say them better, and that while God may welcome my willingness to play a part, this show will go on with or without me, for as long as God has breath to bring more players to life. Today I will take a break from trying to save the world and enjoy my blessed swath of it instead. I will give thanks for what is instead of withholding my praise until all is as it should be. If I get good enough at this, I may even be able to include my sorry self in the bargain. *O men and women everywhere, glorify the Lord, praise him and highly exalt him forever.*

As I rounded the corner on my first front porch church service with the congregation of creation, I framed an apology to all the people who had ever told me they were not in church the previous Sunday because the weather had been so nice. At the time, I had judged them for shirking their duty to worship in community. I had thought that they needed to be where I was, meeting their own responsibilities for keeping Grace-Calvary going. Clearly, I had forgotten that people are not the only creatures who glorify the Lord. I think I had also envied the freedom of those who chose to keep the Sabbath in their own ways. On the first Sunday after I left church, the irony was hard to miss. If one day without work had that much holiness in it for me, then what else had I missed while I was laboring for the Lord?

G etting dressed in the morning was the hardest part. For years, I had spent no more than two minutes in my closet, where a row of black, long-sleeved clergy shirts hung next to a row of compatible skirts, suits, or jumpers. All I had to do was mix and match, attach the white plastic collar, and I was on my way. Some mornings I did not even look in the mirror. Of course I had stacks of sweats and jeans for working around the farm, and another closet downstairs with bright clothes in it that I wore only on vacation, but for six days every week I spent as little time on my wardrobe as a nun.

The price of this ease was the way my uniform shaped other people's responses to me. Those with no frame of reference sometimes took it for a fashion statement. A man standing in line with me at a grocery store in Atlanta once asked me if I were headed to a costume party as a cross-dressing priest. In Clarkesville, the collar had a more sobering effect, especially among church members. When people saw it in public, they shifted from normal gear into the most reverent gear they could find. I was a reverend, after all. They talked about things that they thought might interest me, such as Sunday school or how the plans for the Vacation Bible School were shaping up. Although I never asked, some explained why they had not been in church lately, while others promised that they would catch up on their financial pledges just as soon as they were able. As well intentioned as such deference was, it was as distancing as a velvet rope in a museum. I had the clear sense that I was supposed to stay on my side of it, where I would not get mixed up in things that were too crude or worldly for me.

I would have thought this had something to do with my gender if I had not heard a clergyman describe the same phenomenon in the small community where he lived. "I am always invited to the Christmas parties," he said, "but never to the New Year's Eve parties. Why is that?" He knew the answer, the same as I did. Who wants a clergyperson leaning on the bar at a bacchanalia? Especially a clergyperson who has heard your confession?

One New Year's Eve many years ago, I was invited to a party at a fancy club in downtown Atlanta. My host was a parishioner whose law firm threw this gala every year, spending more on boiled shrimp and ice sculptures than I made in a month. I am not sure what possessed him to invite me, but I decided to rise to the occasion. Ed dusted off his tuxedo. I made an appointment with a hairdresser. Since everything in my closet was black, gray, or black with gray stripes, I borrowed a royal blue dress with sequins on it from my younger sister, who was a lawyer. The neck was high and the sleeves were long, but the thing still sparkled. I loved it almost as much as I loved the idea that I was the kind of person who could wear it, but as soon as I handed my coat to the coat check person I knew that I was wrong.

I did not know how to stand in the dress or where to put my hands. I could not think of anything to say that went with the dress. All of the things I was used to talking about went with the serious clothes in my closet, while this dazzling outfit called for something that Billie Holiday might say, or Dorothy Parker at least. When I saw people I knew from church, I saw my own discomfort mirrored in their faces. Seeing their priest in a blue sequined dress at a New Year's Eve party was like running into their dentist in a Speedo at the beach. They could hardly look at me. I asked Ed if we could go home early, and the following year I helped design a New Year's Eve liturgy that took place at church instead.

The gap between my public persona and my pastoral role was always one of the more disorienting aspects of my job. In public, people treated me like the Virgin Mary's younger sister. They watched their language. They shielded me from their darker natures. They guarded my purity. But sooner or later many of them needed a pastor, and when that time came neither of us could afford the pretense of my innocence any longer. Like most clergy, I know how to post bond, lead an intervention, commit someone to a mental health care facility, hide a woman from her violent husband, visit an inmate on death row, and close the eyes on a dead body. One summer when a frightened murder witness showed up at the church door I even learned how to arrange an appointment with the district attorney for testimony before a grand jury.

I also know how to listen to far less spectacular stories about the kinds of things that routinely upend human lives. Whether the subject is divorce, job loss, serious illness, troubled children, or aging parents, these confessions can expose such raw places in the people who make them that the anonymity of the old-fashioned confessional makes a great deal of sense to me. If I had used one of those, then the people I listened to would not have had to let on that we knew each other, even if we learned to recognize one another's voices. We would still have been able to see one another around church without having to acknowledge what had passed between us. While some people develop an attachment to the pastor who has witnessed their grief or fury, others are so ashamed that they never again seek counsel. Having found someone kind enough to accept their radioactive waste, they have no intention of ever going back to visit.

To survive in parish ministry, one learns not to take such things personally. When I first started out, I welcomed all attachments to me as positive responses to my ministry and all avoidances of me as invitations to try harder. Gradually I learned that both attitudes had more to do with things that happened in people's lives a long, long time ago than they had to do with me. I was in the right role, was all. I was the one whose job was to take care of people, and when I failed I took my place in the long line of unsuccessful caretakers who had come before me. A bishop with decades of ministry behind him finally supplied me with the insight that became my mantra. "The people you think love you don't love you as much as you think they love you," Frank said to me, "and the people you think hate you don't hate you as much as you think they hate you."

This was easier to accept once I was no longer face-to-face with them. I could also see more clearly where my role had cut into my soul. I needed the soul's wisdom to do my work. I needed its compassion. But I had too often failed to set it loose in its own pasture at night, where it could kick its heels and roll in the dirt. I had kept my soul so hitched to the plow that it stood between the traces even after the harness was off, oiled, and hung on the wall.

In my role, I could act out of my best nature for hours at a time. I could produce kindness when all I felt was fatigue. I could present patience when circumstances warranted irritation. I could shine like the sun until long after dark when I needed to, but my soul did not operate on a solar calendar. My soul operated on a lunar calendar, coming up at a different time every night and never looking the same way two nights in a row. Where my role called for a steady circle of bright light, my soul waxed and waned. There were days when I was as full as a harvest moon and others when not so much as a sliver appeared in the sky. My soul's health depended on the regular cycle of these phases. I needed the dark nights that gave the stars their full brilliance as much as I needed the nights when the moon shone so brightly that I could make shadow puppets with my hands. The problem with the collar was that it did not allow for such variations. It advertised the steady circle of light, not the cycles, so that it sometimes scorched my neck.

I do not think that I was the only one who suffered from too much sun in church. One thing that had always troubled me was the way people disappeared from church when their lives were breaking down. Separation and divorce were the most common explanations for long absences, but so were depression, alcoholism, job loss, and mortal illness. One new widow told me that she could not come to church because she started crying the moment she sat down in a pew. A young man freshly diagnosed with AIDS said that he stayed away because he was too frightened to answer questions and too angry to sing hymns. I understood their reasoning, but I was sorry that church did not strike these wounded souls as a place they could bring the dark fruits of their equally dark nights.

Some of them returned when their moons had filled out a little and others did not, but even people in no apparent crisis seemed to suffer from the full-sun effect. As enjoyable as it could be to spend a couple of hours on Sunday morning with people who were at their best, it was also possible to see the strain in some of the smiles, the effort it took to present the most positive, most faithful version of the self. Sometimes I could almost read the truth written out above people's heads: "Please don't believe me. This is only a shard of who I really am." The cost of the pretense was the loss of the real human texture underneath, but since we all thought that was what was expected of us, that was what we delivered.

One of my favorite mornings at Grace-Calvary was the one when Andy showed up to read scripture at the early service with a front tooth missing. His cap had fallen off during the night, he explained, when I asked him what had happened. Air whistled through his remaining teeth when he spoke. As hard as I worked to keep my eyes away from the hole, they kept straying back. Anyone else would have called in sick or arranged a substitute, but Andy could have cared less. He was the guy who showed up to shovel the sidewalks on Sunday mornings after a heavy snow, staying for the service even if there were only the two of us and no heat. He was the guy who climbed three ladders to knock the wasp's nest out of the bell tower, while his German shepherd watched from the cab of his truck below. He was also the guy who could get into a shouting match with me over how the church was spending his pledge, but Andy's real human texture was always on display. When he stood up to read scripture that morning with a lisp as pronounced as his devotion, I loved him entirely.

I knew clergy like him too, who never let their collars cut off their air, but they seemed to possess some force of character that I did not possess. I had set out to wear a collar in the first place because I thought it would mark me as someone committed to going all the way with God. *Will you seek and serve Christ in all persons, loving your neighbor as yourself?* My initial answer had been yes, I would. I would give myself completely to that ministry. I wore my collar the way I wore my wedding ring, as a symbol of my vows. But, as I had suspected when I first opened the box from Wippell's, what the collar symbolized to other people was not under my control. In the same way that a prisoner's stripes identified someone with a criminal record, a collar identified someone with divine aspirations, which did not always bode well for the person who wore it.

While I knew plenty of clergy willing to complain about high expectations and long hours, few of us spoke openly about the toxic effects of being identified as the holiest person in a congregation. Whether this honor was conferred by those who recognized our gifts for ministry or was simply extended by them as a professional courtesy, it was equally hard on the honorees. Those of us who believed our own press developed larger-than-life swaggers and embarrassing patterns of speech, while those who did not suffered lower-back pain and frequent bouts of sleeplessness. Either way, we were deformed.

We were not God, but we spent so much time tending the God-place in people's lives that it was easy to understand why someone might get us confused. As Christians, we were especially vulnerable, since our faith turned on the story of a divine human being. Those who became ordained were not presented with Moses or Miriam as our models, so that we could imagine ourselves as flawed human beings still willing to lead people through the wilderness. We were not presented with Peter or Mary Magdalene as our models, so that we could imagine ourselves as imperfect disciples still able to serve at our Lord's right hand. Instead, we were called to fill in for Jesus at the communion table, standing where he once stood and saying what he once said. We were called to preach his gospel and feed his sheep. We were, in other words, presented with Jesus himself as our model, so that most of us could only imagine ourselves disappointing everyone in our lives from God on down.

The vocational crisis that put an end to my wearing a collar every day exposed the pale neck of my lunar soul. My real human texture came out of hiding for the first time in years, and I had so much catching up to do that I was not always pleasant to be around. I rode my mood swings as far as they would go instead of trying to get them to stop. I yelled a lot and practiced colorful language. I went to the grocery store in blue jeans and spent too much money on red clothes.

Like an Amish youth entering my *rumspringa*, I embarked on a period of running around on my faith community. I let down my hair, although as my friend Martin says about himself, I do not have very long hair. My experiment, such as it was, had more to do with my identity than my behavior. Both as a priest and as the rector of a parish, I had been given my identity for so long that I hardly knew how to start making up one of my own.

For fifteen years, my clericals had been like my car. Once I was inside of them I did not think about them much, although my identification with them was complete. Back before Saabs were well known in the United States, I drove one that was shaped like a leaf beetle. These were the same cars that Swedish police and mail carriers drove, which gave those of us who drove them a certain sense of superiority. In the event of mud, sleet, or snow, our front-wheel drive took us places no Buick would ever dream of going. Until then, we had a look that set us apart from every other car on the road.

When I passed other Saabs on the highway, we flashed our headlights at one another in recognition. We knew that our headliners would sooner or later begin to sag because Saab used glue made from reindeer hooves. We also knew that if our cars broke down out of town we might have to wait three days for a new water pump to arrive, but that almost never happened until the second hundred thousand miles. Meanwhile we enjoyed the camaraderie of our oddness. There were not many of us, which meant that people noticed us, and even when they did not notice us we noticed one another.

One day when I needed to take a big dog to the vet I borrowed Ed's car. After adjusting all of his mirrors and getting the feel of his clutch, I pulled out of the driveway and headed for the highway. He had a better sound system than I did, of which I was making full use when I saw a Saab heading toward me. Since making the first move was part of the game, I hurried to flash my headlights and waited to be recognized. The approaching Saab did not return my signal. Was the driver unfriendly or simply uninitiated? I flashed my lights again. The driver did not even look at me as he sailed right past, which was when I remembered I was driving an Audi.

After I left church, the same thing happened to me on foot. Cruising the aisles at the Winn-Dixie, I did not get the same looks that I was used to. When I gave strangers the smile that went with the clerical collar, most of them sailed right past, which was how I remembered that I was wearing street clothes. While people I knew still flashed their lights, we treated one another as gingerly as onetime lovers who had resolved to remain friends. But such encounters happened less often than I expected in a town as small as Clarkesville. As it turned out, there were a whole lot of people I did not know, including teenaged cashiers at the hardware store who treated me as indifferently as they treated everyone else, and motorcyclists at the filling station who did not clean up their language when I pulled up to the pump.

While there was a certain thrill in discovering how people talk when they do not think there is an ordained minister around, I was shocked to discover how civilians are treated, especially when they are women. When I stood at a busy store counter waiting to be helped, I watched the clerk attend to every man in the vicinity before turning at last to me. When Ed and I met someone new at a concert, I learned to stand quietly while our new acquaintances tried to find out what Ed did for a living. Without my collar, I became invisible. Nothing set me apart from any other middle-aged woman who had not bothered to color her hair. But that was what I had wanted, wasn't it? Not to be set apart? As I fought the instinct to flash my lights, I tried to remember that was what I had wanted.

If my second loss upon leaving church was the ease of a given identity, then my second gain was the fellowship I felt with a far wider swath of humanity once I took my collar off. As on the night of my rebaptism in the swimming pool, I found myself bobbing in the water with everyone else instead of standing on the cement tossing life preservers. There was shame in this at first, as I watched other people step in to fill the role of lifeguard, but I was so sure I wanted to stay in the water that I resolved to get used to it. When I did, the shame changed to something closer to humility. I was neither as good as I hoped I might be nor as bad as I feared. I was simply another of God's beggars, grateful to have found my way into the pool.

I finally wrecked my old Saab on the Cross-Bronx Expressway. A bunch of white bottles lying in the road turned out to be a spilled carton of motor oil that sent cars sliding in all directions. When the tow truck driver retrieved my green hood from the center lane, it had the twin treads of a tractor-trailer running right across it. To this day, I do not know whether to remember that car as the one in which I almost lost my life or the one in which my life was saved.

In the normal course of things, clergy leave churches in order to go to other churches. Since I was staying in Clarkesville, I had to figure out another way to get some distance on Grace-Calvary. While my friend at Clarkesville Baptist Church routinely looked out upon one or two of his retired predecessors sitting in the congregation, the Episcopal Church does not handle the transition of its leaders in that way. Once you are gone, you are gone. You find somewhere else to worship on Sundays, and if any of your former parishioners approach you about doing things they do not feel comfortable asking their new pastor to do, you find a gentle way to say no. Before I left Grace-Calvary, I wrote what one church member called my "ultimatum letter," explaining why I would not be available to do baptisms, weddings, or funerals even though I was remaining in the area. Right or wrong, I explained, the accumulated wisdom of our tradition says that it is hard for a congregation to latch onto a new pastor with the old one still hanging around.

For this reason, I did not set foot back inside Grace-Calvary Church until a woman I cared about died. Another priest was set to conduct the funeral. All I wanted was to be there in street clothes. Delaying my arrival so that I would not have to talk to too many people, I reached the porch of the church just as one of the ushers began tolling the bell. Rushing past him, I stepped into the narthex of the church, where a second usher blocked my path. "It's full," he whispered, "but there may still be a few seats up there." He pointed up the steep steps leading to the balcony, where I knew fifteen or twenty folding chairs flanked the old pipe organ.

He said it kindly enough, but he might as well have been a bouncer in a nightclub for all the affront I felt. Refused entrance to the dance floor I had once ruled, I climbed the steps to the balcony, almost as stung by the loss of my old privileges as I was embarrassed to have forgotten that they were no longer mine. There was no seat waiting for me up front any longer. From now on I would have to arrive early and hunt for a place like everyone else.

This was easier to remember in churches where I had never worked. In the months following my resignation from Grace-Calvary, I decided to attend an Episcopal church in a neighboring county where a friend of mine was rector. The forty-five-minute drive was tedious, especially since I lost the NPR signal in the mountains before I was halfway there, but my friend could not have been more welcoming. He even invited me to preach one Sunday so that I would not lose my serve, which was how I learned that I did not belong there. My sermon was so weak that I punched up the delivery to try and save it, but I could not strike a single spark in the eyes of those who were listening to me. Both they and I knew that I did not love them. How could I? I did not even know them. At the door after the service, a sweet-faced woman shook my hand.

"Thank you for coming," she said, bunching her shoulders into a small shrug. "It was fine, I guess. It's just that we love Sam."

After that I tried an Episcopal church twenty minutes in the other direction, where I knew more people. Arriving ten minutes before the hour, I chose a pew on the back right side and sat close to the aisle next to a stuffed brown bear. Instinct had led me to the pew for restless children, but so far I had the bear all to myself.

As I waited for the service to begin, people arrived to take their places. While I sat looking at the backs of their heads, I felt the anticipation growing in my body, like muscle memory in a limb that is gone. Those moments just before the liturgy began were always packed with tension. Had all of the lectors showed up? Were the acolytes' robes clean? Those were the moments when people chose to give me prayer requests I would never remember, when I realized that I had not counted the pages of my sermon to make sure that they were all there. In sixty seconds it would be too late to do anything about these things. When the organist struck the first note of the first hymn, I would loosen the last rope and the boat would leave the dock. Sailing down the aisle behind the crucifer, I would watch the heads on either side of me bow before the cross. Seeing them in profile, I would begin to tally who was there. Soon I would stand before them, looking out at their sea of shining faces, and it would be the best moment of the morning so far.

The boat left without me that morning. I bowed before the cross, the celebrant walked past me, and when he turned around to say the opening sentences I realized that I had been robbed. He could see all of our faces, but the only one I could see was his. He had the best seat in the house — reserved, up front, with plenty of elbow room and a prime view of the human scenery. No wonder most clergy do not see anything wrong with the way most churches are arranged. From the rear all you can see is that most people do not think to comb their hair in the back, which leaves you wondering whether you remembered to do that yourself.

There is also a difference between singing hymns that you yourself carefully chose and singing hymns that someone else chose. For me, at least, familiarity is not the point as much as message, since sung words affect me in ways that said words do not. Where sermons slide off, hymns sink in. Days later, I can be minding my own business, doing something as secular as sweeping the kitchen floor or balancing the checkbook, when I begin to hum a hymn tune. If I stop to identify it, I can usually recover the words, which are often so pertinent to my situation that they arrive like Priority Mail from God. For this reason, I loathe singing hymns that rhyme *blame* and *shame,* or *foes* and *oppose,* so that I cannot shake the sharp tacks of their message from my mind, but when someone else is choosing the hymns, there is no telling what will slide down the chute into my subconscious. This should by all rights increase my sympathy for those who once endured my hymn choices, but it does not. All it increases is my wish to be in charge.

I was, however, no longer in charge. I was no longer leading the prayers, reading the gospel, preaching the sermon, or breaking the bread. I was no longer wearing special clothes or sitting in a reserved seat. I was not the focus of anyone's attention. I was not essential to anything that was going on. Instead, I was sitting in a pew wearing a nice dress following someone else's directions, and this was not going particularly well for me. At the passing of the peace, I embraced the woman who had slid in next to me.

"Wow," I said, "things look really different from back here." She smiled a gnostic smile.

"You're used to being *in* the play," she said without irony. "Now you're *watching* the play. Welcome to the audience."

I hardly know what to call this loss. Like the loss of my job, it involved the loss of identity. I no longer had a prime place to sit or a big role to play. I had also lost the beloved community with whom I had worshiped for five and a half years. But I think that the word I am looking for, which I am also loath to use, is *power*. I had lost my institutional power, which offered me the first of many lessons in the difference between church teachings and the view from the pew.

The church teaches—I myself have taught—that *liturgy* means "the work of the people." The priest serves as the people's representative in worship, who does on their behalf what they are all called to do. When the priest prays, proclaims the gospel, or blesses bread and breaks it before handing it around, he or she is standing in for the priesthood of all believers, who are called to do the same sorts of things in their own lives in the world. Worship is a communal practice, I have explained to hundreds of inquirers. Although there may only be one person standing behind the altar, we are all offering our thanksgiving to God.

Maybe so, but there is no denying that it feels much truer when you are the one behind the altar than it does when you are sitting eight rows back on the right, speaking only when you are spoken to while someone else carries the play.

Behind the altar, I felt as if I were standing in a concentrated beam of pure glory. Perhaps it was the collected energy of the gathered community focused on one spot, or perhaps it was the presence of the bright, invisible God. Whatever it was, it could make the hair stand up on my arms. Pronouncing sacred words on behalf of sixteen, sixty, or six hundred other people multiplied the power of the words just that many times so that the language made my head swim as it came out of my mouth.

When I raised my hands in the air above the bread and the wine, I could sense the ancient weight of the gesture. Who stands like that outside of church anymore, save dancers and children? Calling the Holy Spirit to come into the elements with my hands held up like that, I felt as if there should be a ring of standing stones behind me instead of the plaster wall of a church, but it did not matter where I was if the Spirit was there. Time and place fell away. I was standing at the only table where that supper had ever been laid, with everyone who had ever longed for it.

When I broke the bread, the smell of wheat and honey made my mouth water. No matter how many times I did it, I could not wait to taste the bread. Then I lifted the chalice of fragrant port wine to my lips, making myself stop with one sip. This rare restraint focused my senses as excess never did. The bridegroom had saved the best until then.

As people made their way toward the altar rail, I came as close as I ever did to seeing who they really were. They were hungry, just like me. They were as helpless as I was to be as whole as God made them to be. They were doing the best they could. They were also praying, most of them, so that they did not look at me. Outstretched hands took the place of up-turned faces. Looking down at them, I could see how each pair of hands told me the story of a life. Whether that life had been short or long, rough or smooth, it was opening up to me then, ready to receive God's food and I — I — got to place the holy bread there in the center of each palm, watching the fingers curl around it as if Jesus himself had given it to them.

When people ask me what I miss most about serving a church, the answer is: *this.* I miss baptisms and funerals, parish picnics and hospital calls, but what I miss most of all is celebrating communion with people I love. I miss being a light-ning rod, conducting all that heat and light not only from heaven to earth but also from person to person. Most of us do not live especially holy lives, after all. We spend most of our time sitting in traffic, paying bills, and being irritated with one another. Yet every week we are invited to stop all of that for one hour at least. We are invited to participate in a great drama that has been going on without us for thousands of years, and one that will go on as long as there is a single player left standing.

If this terrific mystery is not apparent to most people sitting in the pews, then there are at least two things wrong. One is that worship has become too tame, and the other is that those who come have stopped bringing their own fire. The two may even be related, but neither is easily solved, nor am I sure that many people want them to be. Tame worship is easier to agree on than any other kind, and bringing fire requires a lot more energy than simply showing up. When life is pretty good and church is pleasant enough, who needs resurrection?

But there may also be something wrong with giving one person so much power, so that the starring role in the drama goes to the same person every week. I did not think about this much when I was one of several clergy on a large church staff, but at Grace-Calvary I felt the heat more keenly. Week after week, I was permitted to stand up in special clothes and talk while everyone else sat quietly and listened. Week after week, they heard the gospel filtered through my sensibilities. On Sunday mornings they sang the hymns I had chosen, and on Wednesday evenings they engaged the topics I had picked. While this situation was relieved somewhat by a couple of fine clergy associates and several gifted parish leaders, I remained aware of my (and their) inordinate power. Once, a man who routinely sent me clippings from the *Christian Science Monitor* included an essay of his own on a topic close to his heart. "We know a lot about what matters to you," he wrote, not unkindly. "I thought you might like to know about something that matters to me."

If I sometimes felt like a hostile parent and my parishioners like overmanaged children, it was not all our fault. We needed a different way of being together before God, shaped more like a circle than a pyramid. We needed to ditch the sheep paradigm. We needed to take turns filling in for Jesus, understanding that none of us was equal to the task to which all of us had been called. We needed to share the power.

When I lost my power, at least three things happened. The first was that I felt a great welling up of tenderness for everyone still trying to make a go out of church the way it was. I felt tender toward the clergy, since I knew that most of them did not feel powerful at all and were in fact baffled by the strong resistance they sometimes roused in their parishioners. I felt tender toward the parishioners, for remaining loyal to churches that revolved far too tightly around the personalities of their ministers. I even felt tender toward myself, for continuing to open myself up to other people's agendas when I came to church to worship God. When I was in charge, I knew nothing about the kind of vulnerability this requires. Now that I know, I understand what an act of courage it can be to trust other human beings to give voice to one's prayers.

The second thing that happened when I lost my power was that I got a taste of the spiritual poverty that is central to the Christ path. Since this virtue has all but vanished from the American church scene, it is often hard to recognize. With so much effort being poured into church growth, so much press being given to the benefits of faith, and so much flexing of religious muscle in the public square, the poor in spirit have no one but Jesus to call them blessed anymore. Yet his way endures as a way of emptying the self of all its goods instead of shoring up the self with spiritual riches. Only those who lose their lives can have them.

Sometimes known by its Greek name, this *kenosis* is captured best in the second chapter of Paul's letter to the Philippians. "Let the same mind be in you that was in Christ Jesus," he writes, "who, though he was in the form of God, did not regard equality with God as something to be exploited, but emptied himself, taking the form of a slave, being born in human likeness." The important thing to notice is that no one emptied this Christ Jesus. He willingly emptied himself, leaving his followers a baffling example of how powerful the surrender of all power can be. While my taste of this truth was admittedly no more than a drop on my tongue, I could still taste it. My new powerlessness in church gave rise to such a riot in my ego that I became freshly aware of how much emptying I had left to do. The wish to be in charge was, among other things, the wish to avoid the pain of not being in charge, of my life or anything else.

The third thing that happened when I lost my power was that my priesthood emptied into the world. As I became a sojourner in congregations where I had no official role, I began to understand that while I had lost institutional power, I was still a priest. No longer tied to one particular community, I began to sense myself part of the far larger congregation of humankind. No longer responsible for one particular altar, I began to see altars everywhere. There are surely as many definitions of priesthood as there are priests, but I have always thought of myself as someone whose job is to recognize the holiness of things and then hold them up to God. When I served one particular congregation, my job was to officiate at the offering of that community's life to God, whether that took place in worship, around a hospital bed, at the soup kitchen, or in the nursery. Over and over, being the priest meant that I was the one who got to set these things on the altar, presenting them to God along with our deep thanks for the privilege of being alive.

After I left church, I did not expect to do this anymore, at least not officially. Then one day while I was waiting in line at the post office, I realized that I could unofficially thank God for every person standing in that line with me, lingering just long enough on each one of them to become aware of another human being as much in need of love as I. When Ed invited me to dig potatoes with him later that afternoon, I sank my hands into the scented earth and held each Yukon Gold up like a communion wafer. While I was shoveling out the horse stall a little later still, I counted the beating hearts on our farm—two horses, four dogs, three cats, three llamas—including Ed and me, that made a congregation of fourteen whose lives I might hold up to God.

Gradually I remembered what I had known all along, which is that church is not a stopping place but a starting place for discerning God's presence in this world. By offering people a place where they may engage the steady practice of listening to divine words and celebrating divine sacraments, church can help people gain a feel for how God shows up—not only in Holy Bibles and Holy Communion but also in near neighbors, mysterious strangers, sliced bread, and grocery store wine. That way, when they leave church, they no more leave God than God leaves them. They simply carry what they have learned into the wide, wide world, where there is a crying need for people who will recognize the holiness in things and hold them up to God.

Although I never found a church where I felt completely at home again, I made a new home in the world. I renewed my membership in the priesthood of all believers, who may not have as much power as we would like, but whose consolation prize is the freedom to meet God after work, well away from all centers of religious command, wherever God shows up.

# CHAPTER

# 14

In the months following my resignation from Grace-Calvary, I spent a lot of time interpreting my decision to people who cared about me. One day I received a long e-mail from a clergy friend I had met seven years earlier in Israel. We were both parish priests back then, spending part of our sabbaticals at Saint George's College in Jerusalem. Bouncing around the Holy Land on the back bench of a tourist bus, we formed a bond based in large part on a shared sense of irreverent humor. When he was elected a bishop some years later, I was relieved that he did not change the way he talked, at least to me. He continued to tell me stories that made me laugh out loud, risking impieties he might otherwise have censored because he knew I was as committed as he was to the Church.

The long e-mail arrived after he learned of my resignation. In it, he was as kind as ever, but the humor was all gone. He wondered how I was doing, he said. He hoped that I would not waste any time finding a spiritual director who might help me through my crisis. He wanted me to know that no matter

how far I felt from God, God was not far from me. Reading
his reassurances, I remembered how much time bishops spend
bandaging clergy who have walked off the edge. In my reply, I
blessed my friend for his concern and told him to relax. I had
not lost my faith. If anything, my decision to leave church was
a bid to live into that faith more fully. When he wrote back, he
was his old self again. He was so immersed in the life of the
Church, he said, that he occasionally forgot that the life of
faith was not always the same thing.

*I'll say.* By fleeing the church to seek refuge in the world, I
had reversed the usual paradigm, and I had to learn my way
around the new one. For half my life, the axis of my world had
run through the altar of a church. I spent most of my time in
church, with church people, engaging in the work of the
church. My view of reality grew from that center. I looked at
life through the windows of the church, using the language I
had learned there not only to describe what I saw but also to
make sense of it. My context was so tightly focused that even
my junk mail was Christian.

Within a matter of weeks, much of that had changed for
me. Without a place to be every Sunday, without a collar to define my identity or a job to lend me institutional power, I
found myself on the outside looking in. This was almost literally true some Sundays, when I wanted to hide in the hedges at
Grace-Calvary until the service started and then rise up just
high enough to get a good look at my old congregation. On a
more symbolic level, it was true every time I came across some
religious certainty that I had previously preached, taught, or
believed and found myself wondering if it were really so. Did

the Nicene Creed really cover all the bases of the Christian story? Was the Bible always the word of God? Freed from defending the faith, I began to revisit what faith really meant to me and found that much of the old center did not hold.

The definition of faith that I heard most often had to do with being certain what you believed. When two girls from the Christian Missionary Alliance Church knocked on my dorm room door during my sophomore year in college, they were certain who God was, what God wanted from them and from me, where they were going to spend eternity, and what I needed to do to join them in heaven. At nineteen, I could not answer any of the questions they asked me from scripture, about how I was going to get across the abyss between God and me. So they drew me a picture on the pad of paper they carried with them, of a cross spanning a chasm. Then they told me exactly how the cross-shaped bridge worked, adding a stick figure on it that they said could be me. Stunned by the sheer volume of the information they possessed about God, I wilted before them, kneeling where they asked me to kneel and saying what they asked me to say. Phrase by phrase, they prompted me in the sinner's prayer, which I hoped might sow the same certainty in me that was so evident in them.

Six months later, I had experienced something I perceived to be the Holy Spirit at work in me. As best I could describe it, it was an illumination of ordinary people, trees, sidewalks, dogs—the world, in a word—so that everything seemed to be lit from within. While I was certain this had happened, I was not certain what it meant. I had read everything the campus Christians had given me to read by then. I had done everything they had told me to do, without arriving at the same confidence that they seemed to possess. I possessed curiosity. I possessed awe. I possessed hope, doubt, and fear, but nothing like certainty about what I believed. When I brought this up in Bible study, the other girls looked at me as if I had just passed gas. Clearly, I was not where I was supposed to be in my walk with God. As my friend Becca once said, "The church answered all my questions while I was growing up, but they also gave me the questions I could ask."

By the time I resigned from Grace-Calvary, I had arrived at an understanding of faith that had far more to do with trust than with certainty. I trusted God to be God even if I could not say who God was for sure. I trusted God to sustain the world although I could not say for sure how that happened. I trusted God to hold me and those I loved, in life and in death, without giving me one shred of conclusive evidence that it was so. While this understanding had the welcome effect of changing faith from a noun to a verb for me, it was an understanding that told me how far I had strayed from the center of my old spiritual map.

Like any other map, mine had both a center and an edge. At the center stood the Church, where good women baked communion bread, ironed altar linens, and polished silver that had been in the church family for generations. Parents presented their children for baptism, and those children grew up with dozens of church aunts and uncles who knew them by name. The Christian education committee recruited Sunday school teachers, the youth group leaders planned pizza parties at the bowling alley, and the choir rehearsed from 6:30 to 8:00 in the parish house on Thursday nights. At the center, some people never picked up a prayer book on Sunday morning because they knew the communion service by heart, and even those who had to look said the Nicene Creed all the way through without leaving any parts of it out. These people at the center kept the map from blowing away.

As it turned out, the edge of the map was not all that far from the center. It was not as if I or anyone else had to take a mule train for three weeks to find ourselves in the wilderness. All we had to do was step outside the Church and walk to where the lights from the sanctuary did not pierce the darkness anymore. All we had to do was lay down the books we could no longer read and listen to the howling that our favorite hymns so often covered up. There were no slate roofs or signs to the restroom out there, no printed programs or friendly ushers. There was just the unscripted encounter with the undomesticated God whose name was unpronounceable — that, and a bunch of flimsy tents lit up by lanterns inside, pitched by those who were either seeking such an encounter or huddling in their sleeping bags while they recovered from one. These people at the edge kept the map from becoming redundant.

According to the Bible, both the center and the edge are essential to the spiritual landscape, although they are as different from one another as they can be. The wilderness of Sinai provided the people of Israel with an experience of God that was distinct from their experience in the Temple in Jerusalem. The Judean desert showed Jesus a side of God's Holy Spirit that was not apparent while magi knelt before his manger in Bethlehem. There is life in both places because the same God is in both places, but they are so different from one another that it is often difficult for people to be one place without wanting to be the other place or to agree that both places really belong on the same map. Much that is certain at the center is up for grabs in the wilderness, while much that is real in the wilderness turns out to be far too feral for the center.

Once, when I attended a workshop on teaching religion, a presenter talked about how he took his students on wilderness trips to give them a taste of life nearer the edge. Whether they went hiking or white-water rafting, the point was to step outside their high-carb comfort zones long enough to encounter the untamed holiness of the wild.

"Excuse me," a member of the audience said, "but are there predators in those places who are above you on the food chain?"

"Well, of course not," the presenter said. "I wouldn't put students in danger like that."

"I wouldn't either," the man in the audience said, "but don't lull them into thinking that they have experienced true wilderness. It's only wilderness if there's something out there that can eat you."

I had been under the care of Mother Church for so long that I had not spent a night out of her sight in years. Now all of a sudden I was outside more nights than I was in, which allowed me to see my mother in a new light. What I saw above all was how well she had provided for me. Lying in the yard all by myself with the spiritual equivalent of a can of cold beans, I looked in through the windows of the church and saw people bathed in golden light eating the meal that I had once shared with them. I saw how Mother Church had not only fed me, clothed me, and housed me but had also given me brothers and sisters to learn to love, even when we did not like each other very much.

I saw how she had taught me the same things that had helped her older children find their way in the world as well as a few that she hoped might keep me safe. *Be careful. Don't leave the yard. No more questions. Because I'm the mother, that's why.* Like any mother, she had also taught me to behave in ways that would reflect well on the family. *Watch your mouth. Tuck in your shirt. Don't play with those children. Wait till your father gets home.* If Mother Church had delivered her advice to me in far more theological language than my own mother had ever used, her intent remained the same. Her job was to take care of me. How else had she come by her name?

Having left the house for the first time in twenty years, I did what most grown children do. I left the yard. I asked lots of questions. I sought out the grown children my mother had taught me not to play with, and in every case I learned that she had not told me the whole truth. While the world was an often frightening place, there was also a great deal of goodness in it. I met people of other faiths and of no faith at all who were doing more "to do justice, and to love kindness" than many of us who know where to find that verse in the Bible. I listened to the stories they told about how badly they had been treated by Christians like me. I read books that had never shown up on any seminary reading list, which raised keen questions about the origins of Christianity and the veracity of scripture that I had never heard anyone address in church.

In the company of Jewish friends, I went way out into the wilderness where I could see my tradition through their eyes instead of my own. They taught me what *messiah* means to a Jew, which is quite different from what it means to most Christians. They taught me things about Second Temple Judaism and first-century life under Rome that enriched my reading of scripture. They gave me a whole new view of Paul. But they also showed me places where the followers of Jesus twisted the truth about Judaism or at least wrote things in such a way that their interpreters could. Once I understood that the gospel writers had not told me the whole truth about the Pharisees, I wondered what else they had not told me. Once I noticed that Luke said things about Paul that Paul denied, I wondered what other quarrels Luke had hidden from my view.

I had never read scripture more carefully in my life, which caused scales to fall from my eyes. Over and over, I discovered how the traditional interpretation of a passage had so determined my reading of it that it was hard for me to see what was actually on the page. For the first time, I noticed that Jesus's frame of reference for himself in Luke 4 was "prophet" and not "messiah" and that the reason his hometown congregation tried to throw him off the cliff was because he proclaimed in their hearing that God did not belong to them. For the first time, I noticed how many books of the Bible are at glorious odds with one another, as Job argues with Proverbs, Ruth with Ezra, Mark with John, and James with Paul.

If none of this had ever come to my attention before, one reason was because I had never had so much time to read before, but another reason was because Mother Church had little interest in the things that were interesting me. Her job was to take care of her family. Why should she get into discussions that might cause them to lose confidence in her? Why encourage them to raise questions for which she had no answers? Even more important, why waste valuable time rehashing things that had been settled centuries ago when there was so much to do around the house right now? I understood her reasons, I really did. I was just looking for some way to stay related to her that did not require me to stay a child.

Because I had left the house, I found less and less to talk about with people who were still happily engaged inside. At clergy gatherings I felt like a single woman listening to dedicated parents discuss day care and home remedies for colic. When I spoke of things that I found fascinating, the resounding silence told me how far I was from the center of the map and how much my distance sounded like disloyalty. Church people who could tell I was in the wilderness were kind enough to invite me back inside the house, but even when I went to visit I did not want to stay. I did not know how to behave anymore. I could no longer speak the lines that I had been given to say. I wanted to go back outside.

If my time in the wilderness taught me anything, it is that faith in God has both a center and an edge and that each is necessary for the soul's health. If I developed a complaint during my time in the wilderness, it was that Mother Church lavished so much more attention on those at the center than on those at the edge.

Because I lived with chickens, I was able to see up close how a mother hen protects her babies. One white hen who sat patiently on twenty-one eggs for as many days finally hatched fourteen chicks, who did their best to stay within the safety of her shadow. In the evening, so many little heads poked out of her feathers that she looked like a condominium. Although I had fed her the whole time she brooded, she withdrew her permission to approach as soon as the eggs hatched. If I came any closer than a yard, she dropped her head and lifted her wings to make herself huge. If I still did not get the message, she attacked, pecking my hand so hard that she drew blood. She was the center of the world for her chicks, who strayed from her at their peril.

Where Mother Church is concerned, those who stray furthest not only forfeit her protection; they may also be shunned as heretics by those who stay home. I have Elaine Pagels to thank for the revelation that the word *heresy* comes from the Greek word for "choice." Early on, before the Christian church had a solid center, a wide variety of people who all called themselves Christian understood the Christ in a wide variety of ways. There were the Ebionites, who understood him as a thoroughgoing Jew. There were the Arians, who understood him as an exemplary human being, and the Docetists, who understood him as God in human disguise.

For almost three centuries, these choices existed in wild disarray. Then the emperor Constantine, in his imperial wisdom, understood that a faith with no center would never anchor his crumbling empire. So he called all the bishops together, fed them lunch, and asked them to say something definitive about the nature of God in Christ. He asked them to sort through the choices and agree on one that the Christian church could go forward with. This required many more lunches and some theological bloodletting as well; but, when the bishops had finished crafting a central confession of Christian faith, those who did not choose this option became known as heretics.

In my closet I have a T-shirt with many of their names on it, which I wore to bed while I was sleeping in the wilderness: Matthew Fox, Hans Küng, Pierre Teilhard de Chardin, Martin Luther, Menno Simons, Meister Eckhart, Joan of Arc, Francis of Assisi, Hildegard of Bingen, Galileo, Copernicus, Peter Abelard, John Scotus Erigena, Tertullian, Origen, Jesus. All of these people made unauthorized choices in their love of God. They saw things they were not supposed to see or said things they were not supposed to say. They wondered about things they were not supposed to wonder about, and when Mother Church told them to stop they did not obey her.

Some of them died for their disobedience while others were locked in their rooms. Still others were sent out of the house and told to never come back. Many of them are spiritual heroes now. At least one of them is revered as the Son of God, but none of them got where they were going without passing through the wilderness first. Given their amazing comebacks, might it be time for people of good faith to allow that God's map is vast, with room on it for both a center and an edge? While the center may be the place where the stories of the faith are preserved, the edge is the place where the best of them happened.

At least that was what I was hoping while I was camping in the wilderness—wondering if I were still a Christian, wondering if the answer to that question depended on what other

Christians said about me or what I said about myself. I wondered if it were time to "renounce my orders," which is the terrible phrase for what Episcopal clergy do when they decide not to be clergy anymore. While my call to leave parish ministry felt as strong to me as my call to enter it had in the first place, "renounce" seemed far too harsh a word. I looked it up in the dictionary, just to be sure, where I found a fourth definition that I liked very much: "in cards, to be unable to follow suit and be forced to play a card from a different suit." Still, I did not do it; I was not yet ready to abandon the idea that I might still be a priest.

I paid visits to the tents of other people camping in the wilderness, including other clergy, who met me with such wordless kindness that I all but decomposed with relief. Some of them were there for reasons much like mine; others had been sent there for crimes that ranged from infidelity to public drunkenness. Sitting around communal campfires with them, confessing our mutual cluelessness about what we might yet be good for in the service of a God whom most of us still loved, I discovered a version of the sinner's prayer that increased my faith far more than the one that I had said years earlier while kneeling by my bed. In this version, there were no formulas, no set phrases that promised us safe passage across the abyss. There was only our tattered trust that the Spirit who had given us life would not leave us in the wilderness without offering us life again.

If another loss in the months following my resignation was the loss of Mother Church, I gained a new attachment to the Holy Spirit, whom I steadfastly experienced as "she." She was unpredictable. She was not safe. She was life-giving. While my heart continued to swell whenever I heard a string of wild geese passing overhead, I also learned to recognize the shrill call of a red-tailed hawk who hunted the fields around my house. I knew that she ate the wide-eyed field mice with the white bellies whom I liked so much, along with any chick that strayed too far from its mother's shadow, but I could not hold that against her. It was the price of her wild beauty, the price I paid to watch her fly.

To see her fold her wings and stoop, falling through the air like a lightning bolt on her prey, was to wonder if Jesus did not see something more like that than "something like a dove" when the heavens split open at his baptism. Maybe the gospel writers did not want to scare the rest of us off, so they left out the part about the talons. I will never know, but I do know that as I emerged out from under the safety of one pair of wings, I was ready to climb onto the back of another. I was even ready to be gripped in her claws, if that was what it took to be carried aloft.

Long before I moved to Clarkesville, I knew my way to the rustic lodge at Unicoi State Park in neighboring White County. Set in deep woods near Anna Ruby Falls, it was a favorite destination for big Atlanta churches on weekend retreats, where people looked forward to cedar in the air, fried catfish on the supper buffet, and quilts on the beds. The promise of these things appeased us as we crept out of town in rush-hour traffic, nosing our way through the visible tunnel of exhaust that hung over the expressway. When the four-lane ended in Gainesville, we took Highway 129 north to Cleveland, then switched to 85 for the last stretch that led past Ma Gooch's restaurant, the lumberyard, and the Yonah Burger stand.

After almost two hours in the car, we knew what we were looking for. Just south of Helen, at the mouth of the Nacoochee Valley, stands an Indian mound topped by a white Victorian gazebo. The sizable knoll sits in the center of a lush pasture full of Holsteins, which makes the place a favorite for photographers. On a sunny day, with Yonah Mountain rising

above the field and the Chattahoochee River sparkling behind it, the black and white of the cows against the vivid
green of the grass and the loud blue of the sky can make you
forget to watch where you are going. Plenty of people pull
over to gape, whether or not they remembered to pack their
cameras.

According to the historical marker, this is a burial mound,
partially excavated by the Smithsonian back when robbing
graves still passed as scientific research. Now fully protected, it
attests to the once-vibrant presence of native people who
knew a life-giving place when they saw one, and who died inside when they were forced to leave. Both Cherokee and
Creek, their troubles began in earnest when they fought on
the wrong side of the Revolutionary War. Because the British
promised them more protection from the settlers who were
invading their tribal lands, the natives joined the royal army of
a king they had never seen. When the king lost, he recalled his
troops to their home across the sea, leaving the native people
to fend for themselves.

Already decimated by war, they were further weakened by
starvation and smallpox, but none of those did them as much
harm as the discovery of gold on Cherokee land. Around 1815,
a Cherokee boy playing in the Chestatee River near
Dahlonega found a yellow pebble that he showed to his
mother. She sold it to a white man. Less than four years later,
the whole territory east of the Chestatee no longer belonged
to the Cherokee. When Andrew Jackson became president in
1828, the removal of the Eastern Band from their ancestral
land moved into high gear. The old Indian fighter worked for

almost two terms to accomplish his goal; he forged the scurrilous New Echota treaty of 1835, which ceded all Cherokee land east of the Mississippi to the United States. Jackson's successor, Martin Van Buren, tried to delay the removal but met with threats from Georgia's governor.

In 1838, armed soldiers rounded up 17,000 Native Americans for a forced march west. The old were prodded with bayonets, the sick stacked in wagons, and the dead buried by the side of the trail. Almost 2,000 people died on the way. Another 2,000 were put in stockades in Oklahoma. A Georgia volunteer, later a colonel in the Confederate Army, said, "I fought through the Civil War and have seen men shot to pieces and slaughtered by thousands, but the Cherokee removal was the cruelest work I ever knew."*

I never learned any of this history in school, where Indians were always spoken of in the past tense. Like most children, I was fascinated by the pictures of painted tepees and half-naked braves on spotted ponies in my social studies books. On the Wednesday before Thanksgiving, I cut feathers out of colored construction paper to make an Indian headdress I wore to the lunchroom. Other children made black pilgrim hats, and we all went out of our way to be nice to each other while we ate pressed turkey and bread stuffing off of our pastel plastic trays. I knew the story of Pocahontas and had even heard of Sitting Bull, but I never imagined that any of their relatives had survived. My teachers spoke of Indians the same way they

---

*Myths of the Cherokee and Sacred Formulas of the Cherokees* by James Mooney (Nashville: Charles and Randy Elder Publishers, 1982), 130.

spoke of dinosaurs, as a thrilling but dangerous species whose inability to adapt had made them extinct.

All these years later, I recognize this as the way that winners often speak of those they have harmed beyond repair. Trying to find some way to live with what we have done, we find solace in the idea that their doom was their own doing. *They were savages, after all. It was them or us.* In the case of Native Americans, we have romanticized those our forebears dispossessed. We wax rhapsodic about their reverence for the earth, their care for the land—without ever offering to give any of it back. One way we do this is by pretending that they no longer exist, at least not in the way that we remember them. The people we might give the land back to wore feather headdresses and rode spotted ponies. They made baskets from river reeds and ground corn between two flat stones. They did not tend gift shops or empty slot machines at the casino up in Cherokee, which effectively lets us off the hook. If we cannot see the Native Americans of our fantasies, then we do not owe them anything because they are not there.

Ed and I had seen the old graves on our place the first day we walked the property, but at the time we did not translate them into deeds, evictions, and removal. It was not until a Cherokee friend came to visit and said he remembered hearing stories about our place from his grandparents that the land began to speak to me. His name was Anacleto. Ed had met him years earlier when they both showed up to protest the excavation of an old burial ground by a land developer. Cleto was a massive man with a noble brow and a ponytail that reached to the middle of his back, who belonged to the Longhair Clan of the Eastern Band Cherokee. When I shook his hand for the first time, Cleto looked at the ground instead of me, which I accepted as a personal favor. His direct gaze was a little more than I could bear at that point.

Soon after they met, Cleto took Ed to the Rosebud Indian Reservation in South Dakota, where a Lakota Sun Dance chief named Elmer Running took everything away from Ed but one wool blanket and set him out on a hill to pray for two days without food or water. When I met Ed at the Atlanta airport, I had a hard time recognizing him. He had shaved his beard, for one thing. He had spent two days naked before God, for another. His eyes were like small suns in the middle of his sun-burned face. He had lost weight. On the way home he said many things, but the one that stuck with me was, "You make church too easy."

By the time we moved to Clarkesville, Ed was deeply involved in Lakota ways. Since these are ways of prayer, he was able to remain Episcopal as well, or perhaps I should say that he was only able to remain Episcopal because of these ways, which offered him concrete means of practicing his faith that teaching Sunday school and singing in the choir did not. While I loved what I saw happening in him, I was also jealous of his new friends and frightened of what might happen if my parishioners learned all that Ed was up to. Even I was undone by some of the stories he told me about talking bugs and helping spirits. I promised to think "angels" whenever he said "spirits," he promised not to invite any church members to a sweat lodge, and we had a truce that we lived with for five years.

Then Cleto came to visit, blessing our place and putting red prayer ties on our gateposts before I knew he was hoping for a spot to hold a North Georgia Sun Dance. Because Cherokee culture is matriarchal, he asked Ed to ask me. Saying yes seemed small enough reparation for what had happened in the past century. It was the only honorable answer as well, but I was still afraid when I said it. By the time the first cars began arriving that July, I was furious as well.

A huge trash container had been parked at the head of my driveway. Blue porta-potties were scattered throughout my beautiful woods. People I did not know were showing up with their children, campers, tents, and coolers, making muddy ruts in my pasture with their trucks and tying their plastic clothes-lines to my trees. By 8:00 the next morning, the neighbors were on the telephone. Could I please ask my guests to slow down on the road? Did they have to come and go at all hours of the night? Speaking of night, what time was the drumming going to stop? Would I give the neighbors some warning next year, so that they could schedule their vacations during the Sun Dance?

I waited for the police to arrive, but they never did. However, a large truck arrived every couple of days to siphon out the porta-potties. "We're number one in the number two business," read the slogan on the driver's door. I watched him lumber down toward the Sun Dance grounds without ever going down there myself. That first year, it was all I could do to stay married. Near the end of the dance, I learned that Ed had invited a church member with Parkinson's disease to the traditional healing round on the third day. The man had come, too, although I never learned what he made of his experience. All I knew was that he had asked someone standing under the arbor with him, "Does Barbara know what's going on down here?" One reason I stayed in the house was so I could answer, "No, I do not."

But, even in the midst of my awful fear and worry, I could sense the blessing settling down over the land. The drum that beat from sunup to sundown began to sound like a heartbeat to me. When it stopped, the branches of the trees seemed to droop a little. The birds murmured in their sleep. When the drum began again the next morning, roosters crowed and breezes stirred the leaves. Through the day people drifted up to the house for firewood, tools, or water. Sometimes I would hear low laughter before I saw them, walking in twos or threes with children trailing behind them. Some had slept so many nights on the ground that they had acquired their own gravity. They moved slowly, as if each step delivered such energy that they were reluctant to lift their feet. They seemed entirely at home in their bodies, entirely at home on the earth, and when they looked at me I saw the same suns that I had seen in Ed's face when he returned home from South Dakota.

After I left church, I lightened up too. No longer frightened of being found out by my congregation, no longer compelled to defend my way of approaching God, I found much to admire in the Native way. I admired the breadth of the community, which included ex-cons and elementary school teachers, firemen and fine artists, who did not identify themselves in these ways but who became known for the gifts they exercised. Some sang, some danced, some cooked, and some kept the fire going, while the Sun Dance chief served as the human tuning fork in their midst. When something was done sloppily or tempers flared, he called everyone to circle up until the way forward was clear again, since songs sung by distracted singers could hurt more people than they helped, and food cooked by an angry cook might burn the roof right off someone's mouth. Cleto once said that his mother's most devastating hot sauce carried a warning on the bottle: "Made while I was mad."

I admired the absence of books, which kept the community focused on living practice instead of scriptural debate. With no central text, the community is centered in the Spirit, or at least in an oral tradition of what living in the Spirit is all about. Ask an elder what happens in a sweat lodge and he will invite you to a sweat lodge. Ask how you are supposed to pray and you will be invited to say a prayer. There are right and wrong ways to do almost everything, but if you do not ask then no one is going to tell you. The idea seems to be that letting you walk into the fire is much more educational than telling you not to walk into the fire.

When I have asked why I have to turn clockwise instead of counterclockwise to be smudged with sage smoke before entering the Sun Dance grounds, or why I am supposed to take off all of my metal jewelry and put it in my pocket, the answer I have most often received is, "Because that is how the spirits showed us to do it." I am Catholic enough to understand this answer and Protestant enough to chafe against it, but as a guest in the Native American tradition I have also learned how practicing these traditions knits the community together in ways that discussing them would not. By valuing direct en-

counters with God more highly than reading about such encounters in a book, the tradition keeps primary experience
alive. The secondary experience of hearing stories about those
encounters and singing songs that celebrate them has great
value of its own, but it is no substitute for the divine meeting.
An elder's job is to facilitate the meeting for those who seek it,
not to serve as a surrogate. An elder's job is to protect the ways
and support those who walk them, so that as few people as
possible get hurt.

I admired the sense of real risk, which kept the community
from imagining God as a stuffed bear. For many Christians I
know, the idea of divine dangerousness went out of fashion
shortly after the book of second Kings was written, or the
book of Amos at the very latest. In the traditional understanding, Jesus put an end to all that by volunteering to satisfy God's
wrath, and since then those who follow him have had nothing
more to fear from God. God has become a great friend who
would like to get to know us all better, if we can find the time.
And if we cannot, then God loves us anyway. "The fear of the
Lord" has become as outdated as an ephod.

This is not true for the Native Americans I know, whose divine meetings have included glimpses of the God who is as far
above them on the food chain as an eagle is to a mouse. When
they will talk about this at all, they do not speak like mice whose
bones have been picked clean. They speak like mice who have
been lifted high into the heavens where they have seen themselves, the world, and the lives they lead with a terrible new
clarity. Set down again, they cannot look at anything the
same way they once did, which means that they cannot live the

same way either. Because their fear has proved to be the means of their transformation, they do not want to get over it. Their time aloft has brought them as close to an eagle as most of them will ever get, which makes their terror appropriate. Their fear of the Lord and the Lord's love of them are two windows on the same reality.

I admired the poverty of the community, which could barely scrape up enough cash to cover expenses, much less to offer gas money to honored guests from far away. While this worked a hardship on those with no other income, it also meant that no time was spent on capital improvements or annual budget requests. When the Sun Dance arbor needed repair, some guys headed to the woods with chainsaws, and when the porta-potty bill came due, there were usually enough one-dollar bills on the blanket to pay it. The food was a miracle of near-biblical proportions, as people showed up with enough venison stew, deep-fried turkey, corn on the cob, and fry bread to feed those who had come with nothing but a half-eaten Snickers bar.

On the last day of the first Sun Dance on Indian Ridge Farm, I carried a big pan of blackberry cobbler down to the grounds for the closing feast. It was my first appearance and I was shy about showing up for the last couple of hours only. Some of the people who greeted me had been there for more than a week, praying all day and sleeping only a few hours on the ground at night. More than a dozen Sun Dancers who had not touched food or water in four days were looking forward to their first meal. While my clean clothes and unmuddied feet marked me as a gatecrasher, no one treated me like one. People came up to thank me for letting them use the land, for

giving them such a good place to pray. Most of them were crying as they said these things to me, which helped me register
how hardened I had become, how used to saying similar things
to other people without letting them get anywhere near my
heart.

I set my pan down and watched while the Sun Dancers
cleared the arbor. A band of muddy children wove through the
crowd, hugging the knees of so many adults that it was impos-
sible to tell who their real parents were. Most of the women
wore bright shawls over long skirts. No one wore shoes. The
smell of the damp, flattened pasture rose straight up from the
ground. Near the south gate of the arbor, a circle of spent
singers sat around the now-silent drum, smoking cigarettes
and telling stories in low, hoarse voices. Right behind them, an
old woman with a long gray braid sat in an aluminum folding
chair with a young man kneeling by her side.

Watching them all, I understood how much I had missed. I
was also glad to be there, especially when I first caught sight of
Ed. He looked a thousand years old, with a bad sunburn and a
four-day beard. The word *wizened* was invented for how he
looked, all except his face. His face leaked light, as if every ray
of sun that had landed on him that week had seeded his pores.
Ed shone, and when he looked at me I felt the beam hit me in
the chest across fifty feet of wet pasture. Then he was gone,
and people started heading toward the arbor with their big
pots full of fragrant stews and vegetables.

I fetched my cobbler and put it on the blanket full of
desserts. Then Cleto called everyone together and said what a
powerful Sun Dance it had been. No one should ever forget

what a privilege it was to pray like that, he said, or how good God was to hear our prayers. He talked about how certain people had been broken by their prayers and put back together again. He told us we had nothing that belonged to us but what we gave to God and that God gave everything back to us again so that we could share it with one another. He told us that we were all related—to each other, to the trees under which we stood, to the ancestors whose bones lay under our feet, to the birds of the air—and that it was way past time to act as if we were. Some people said "Aho" as he spoke, while others shifted from foot to bare foot with their eyes on the food.

I felt like someone who had strolled into the feeding of the five thousand on a casual walk around the lake. The meal looked wonderful, but I had not deserved it. I had slept in a soft bed with four pillows the night before. I had eaten Cheerios for breakfast, taking a hot shower while the cobbler browned in the oven. I had never prayed as hard or as long as even a first-year Sun Dancer, and yet here I was getting ready to enjoy the final feast. So when Cleto asked me to offer the blessing, I felt seriously dizzy. Where was I going to get the words to say in front of this crowd? Why should any of them bow their heads with someone who had just showed up?

Cleto's timing left no room for more than about two exquisitely self-conscious questions like this, leaving me no recourse but to speak from my struck heart—or as near to that spot as I could get—which means that I do not remember one word I said. The only word I remember is "Aho," which is what the people said when I finished. Then I turned with them to the meal spread across four tablecloths, which the Sun Dancers served to everyone else before taking one bite for themselves. All ate and were filled, and when we were finished I took home twelve baskets full of broken pieces at least, including the butt ends of my own gladly devoured heart.

# CHAPTER
## 16

With the new year on the horizon, my three months of unemployment were nearing their end. I had cleaned most of my closets, thinned most of my file cabinets, and answered most of my mail. More important, the load on my heart had begun to ease. Day by day I felt my soul rising through the murky currents of the past year toward a brighter, warmer place. This part did not feel like my doing, although I knew that slowing down had helped me to recover.

Like many ambitious people, I had developed a dependence on adrenaline. I could get so much done when my anxiety was in the red zone that I learned to live right on the edge of panic, in that optimum zone between alarm and collapse. It was my version of running hurdles and I was good at it. As long as I kept moving quickly, there was a great deal I did not have to feel. Sadness and loss were slow movers, along with bewilderment and doubt. Every time I heard them breathing behind me, I put on a burst of speed. But when the tears started leaking out of me on Sunday mornings at Grace-Calvary, I could not find my stride anymore. My feelings caught up with me and escorted me off the track.

After a couple of months of hearing what they had to say, I lost my taste for speed. I could sit still for twenty minutes without fearing my head would explode. I could even want twenty more. A dozen holy Sabbaths had taught me that God could carry on without my help for one day at least. While this knowledge put a dent in my sense of self-importance, it was welcome knowledge. When I took a deep breath, I could feel the energy run all the way to my toes. This was a different rush from the one that adrenaline gave me. When the air came back out of me again, it did not emerge like air escaping through the pinched neck of a rubber balloon. It emerged as the sigh of a rested person, which I had not been for quite some time.

I had thought I would be ready to get back to work by December, but I was wrong. I so loved the rhythm of waking with the sun, working at my own speed, and taking time to visit the chickens every day that the thought of keeping a schedule again filled me with dread. After so many weeks removed from public view, I also shrank from the prospect of being looked at again. Perhaps only deep introverts or people recovering from long illnesses can grasp such reticence, but it really does take a lot of energy to withstand human inspection.

The last time I had avoided it for so long was during my one and only sabbatical, which I spent traveling from Asia Minor to Africa. I lived the last month at a small retreat center near Kakamega, Kenya, in what is left of the rain forest east of Lake Victoria. During the day I straightened out linen closets, patched worn quilts with scraps cut from my host's old silk ties, and wrote long handwritten letters to people back home while chimney sweeps flew in and out of the windows of the room where I was sitting. At night I read whole books by the golden glow of a generator-driven lamp, and when the generator went off at 10:00 PM, by the light of three wax candles that smelled of honey.

While I heard drums in the forest and saw people walking with machetes on the road, I spoke with no more than the same five people every day. The nearest telephone was a twenty-five-minute drive away, in the same town as the post office and the grocery store. When I rode in once a week to shop with Corky, we finished in record time since there was only one kind of milk, one kind of cereal, one kind of rice, and one kind of bread in the little market that we frequented. I never knew how he procured the red wine that we drank with dinner, but we wrapped the empty bottles in newspaper and hid them in the garbage can since good Kenyan Christians do not drink.

When my time there was up, I cried the whole first hour of the ride to the airport. Back home, I realized how many survival skills I had lost during my time away. The mail came too often. The ringing telephone drove me mad. On my first trip to the grocery store, I abandoned my cart in the cereal aisle, utterly overwhelmed by how many kinds of oatmeal there were. Walking out of the store empty-handed, I felt half a dozen pairs of eyes on me, which stung me as badly as a swarm of buzzing bees.

Eventually I remembered how to shut all of these things out, by numbing myself to the vast majority of them. I stopped

flinching when city buses zoomed past me while I was standing on a street corner waiting for the light to change. I grew
back the nerve required to cross three lanes of traffic in a compact car when my highway exit appeared. I remembered how
to handle myself at large gatherings of talking people, and how
to spill excess information when my brainpan was already
overfull.

I learned to withstand human inspection again, but after I
left church I fell back into my rain forest ways. How would I
face twenty-five college students in less than a month's time,
when going to the grocery store was all I could presently manage? How could I ever wear pantyhose again? Preparing a syllabus seemed like the natural first step. I would choose the
books for my world religions course, decide how I wanted to
teach it, and write up a road map that I could follow if I lost
my way.

"Religion 101: Religions of the World," I typed at the top of
a fresh page. This was the class I would teach twice my first
semester and at least once every semester thereafter. In fifteen
weeks, I would cover Hinduism, Buddhism, Confucianism,
Taoism, Shinto, Judaism, Christianity, and Islam, for a grand
total of three hours each on the major wisdom traditions of
the world. Since I had never tried this before, it seemed entirely possible to me. Plus, I had visited countries where each
of those traditions was dominant. All I really had to do was
stay two weeks ahead of the students.

Since I was the only faculty member in religion, I would also
be responsible for teaching Introduction to the Bible, Introduction to Christian Theology, Life of Jesus, and Life of Paul.

As often as I had presented these subjects devotionally at church, I had never taught them academically before. While the prospect of doing this was daunting, it was also exciting to me. One of the most redemptive features of my new job was the clarity of the expectations. I was to teach a set number of students a set body of material. I was expected to spend time in the library in order to do this. I was expected to attend professional meetings in order to continue my own education. I was expected to make a distinctive contribution in my field. After years of stealing hours to read and begging time for study leave, this was like being made to lie down in green pastures, beside still waters that restored my soul.

"Spring 1998," I typed in the top right-hand corner. As a priest, I was used to typing "Epiphany 1998" or "Easter 1998" but never "Spring 1998." For twenty years, I had lived on the church calendar, where each season had its own color and mood. While the calendar from Pence Seed & Feed told me that the date was December 17, I knew it was the third week of Advent, the deep blue season of darkening days that preceded the white feast day of Christmas. Soon after the earth turned back toward the sun at the winter solstice, Mary's labor pains would begin. When her son was born, his cries would call the dawn to come sooner every morning—but not yet. As yet, she was heavily expectant. She stayed on her poky donkey, trusting the journey to deliver her in due time.

After twenty years' worth of Advents, this was not just a season on a calendar but a season of my soul. Having come through the dark, fertile wilderness of the past several months, I was ready to turn my face to the light. I was ready to make my way back to a new center, which would be a classroom this time instead of a church. Checking the academic calendar, I discovered that the first day of class would fall on the tenth day of Christmas (ten lords a leaping). "Thursday," I typed, "Introduction and Course Overview."

From now on, the feast days on my working calendar would not be Epiphany or Easter but Spring Break and Graduation. My longest days would no longer be Saturdays and Sundays but Tuesdays and Thursdays, which would mean canceling classes if I wanted to attend clergy events scheduled during the week. On Maundy Thursday, when diocesan priests renewed their ordination vows at the cathedral, I would be giving a quiz on Judaism under the fluorescent lights of 312 Daniel Hall.

Like most church people, I was free to remember what date it was on the church calendar, but I was no longer free to bend my whole day around it. I would live by two calendars at least, making the same compromises that everyone else made and feeling the same pull between two disparate ways of marking time. Fortunately for me, the academic calendar was as tidal as the church calendar, with low and high times arriving at regular intervals.

While I knew that some professors kept their records on computer programs, I wanted a grade book that I could hold in my hand. In it, I would not only keep attendance but also write notes that would help me remember students' names ("redhead on back row," "baseball cap with flames"). In pencil, I would record scores for quizzes, papers, group presentations, and participation, and at the end of the term I would do the math with the help of a small calculator. Those who missed more than three classes would lose points for not being there, as would those who were chronically tardy.

Never, in all my years of Christian education, had I ever dreamed of holding people accountable to such a degree. Because church attendance is entirely voluntary, so is church education. Sunday school teachers do the best they can with those who show up, deciding how much wisdom for life they can pack into the forty-five minutes they have with their students each week. In the case of adults, this often takes the shape of a short discussion of the Bible readings for the week, on the assumption that adults have already been formed in the faith. In the case of children, the process is more complicated.

Many of the parents I knew took their children to church in hopes of immunizing them against drugs, early sex, teen suicide, drunk driving, and lives of general aimlessness. While freely admitting that they did not know how to speak with their children about God, these mothers and fathers trusted that Sunday school teachers did know how to do that. Sometimes they were right and sometimes they were wrong, but with less than an hour each week there was only so much that any teacher could do. Making Sunday school fun was the important thing so that children would want to come back, even if that meant letting them play Red Rover in the yard instead of teaching them the Beatitudes.

One way or the other, most of the children had left by the time they were thirteen. Twelve was the traditional age for confirmation in the Episcopal Church, when adolescents were invited to confirm the promises made for them at their baptisms. It was their turn to decide, we told them. We had spoken for them when they could not speak for themselves, choosing membership in Christ's body for them the same way we chose warm clothes and nourishing food for them. On the verge of adulthood, they now had the choice. Did they desire to live the Christian life?

Since it is difficult to say no to a question like that, most of them said yes. When the bishop came for his annual visitation, they lined up before him for the laying on of hands. Calling each of them by name, he dipped his thumb in holy oil and made the sign of the cross on their foreheads. Then he clapped his big hands down on their heads and summoned the Holy Spirit to descend upon them, making them fit servants of the living God.

Afterward there was a big party in the parish hall, which many of those young people mistook for graduation. The first adult decision that some of them made was to not attend church anymore, which helped explain why so many grown-ups held adolescent views of faith. Sixth grade was as far as they had gotten in their schooling, which meant that many of them lived the rest of their lives as spiritual twelve-year-olds.

Typing my syllabus, I wondered how much different church might have been if I had been expected to give grades. *How many absences do we get? Will this be on the final exam?*

"Course Requirements," I typed, spelling them out one by one: attendance, reading, writing, field trips, group presentations, exams. It was like planning a trip to some place I had never been, with twenty-five people trusting me to know where I was going. I did not know where I was going, but I was eager to start.

My first class at Piedmont College was scheduled for Tuesdays and Thursdays at 8:00 AM, the Siberia of the school week. Even now, I vividly recall my first 8:00 AM class at Emory College thirty years ago: the dank basement room with clanking radiators, the stark fluorescent lights, the musky smell of wet wood when I woke up with my face flat on my desk beside a small pool of drool.

Of the subject matter I recall nothing, nor of the professor. All I remember is the physical agony of trying to maintain consciousness for an hour and fifteen minutes with the entire gravity of the earth pulling my head down toward the satiny surface of my desk. I tried adjusting my posture. I tried sticking a sharpened pencil in the pads of each of my fingers. I even tried taking notes, but the sucking power of sleep was too great for me. Over and over I lost the good fight, waking up to the sound of chalk screeching on the blackboard with no idea how long I had been out.

I do not recall ever wondering when I was nineteen how this affected my professor. Almost thirty years later, it was payback time. I spent a small fortune on things that I thought might keep my students awake. I purchased a boom box on which I could play world music CDs. I stockpiled all the religious relics I had brought back from other countries: Turkish prayer rugs, Tibetan bells and drums, Thai Buddhas, Greek icons. I composed crossword puzzles that employed key terms from the vocabulary lists in the textbook, and I rented videos in which a British man with very long sideburns traveled around the world interviewing people of various faiths.

My classroom needed all the help it could get. Two dozen tan plastic chairs with Formica desktops were scattered haphazardly across a linoleum floor. One of the fluorescent tube bulbs overhead flickered in the acoustic tile ceiling, making a buzzing sound like the whine of a small drill. A rack of ancient maps stood near the blackboard, which was so slick with age that chalk slid right off it. The first map, of India, showed no sign of Bangladesh. Sri Lanka was still labeled as Ceylon, and Myanmar as Burma. Lifting the heavy page to see what else was underneath, I tipped the whole rack backward and sent it crashing to the floor. I would have to work on my technique before the students arrived.

As a priest, I was trained in the preparation of sacred space. The altar hangings, the linens, the flowers, and the candles were all as important to worship as the words and the songs. When people walked into a space that had been carefully prepared, they were more likely to surrender themselves to it, trusting that whoever cared so much for the room might also care for them. At Grace-Calvary, I had counted on members of the altar guild to polish the silver, iron the linens, arrange the flowers, and trim the candlewicks so that people walked into a gleaming space that smelled of spray starch and chrysanthemums on Sunday mornings. At Piedmont, all I could smell were the old coffee cups in the trash can as I straightened the desks and shoved the map rack behind the door. Although I knew that a college class was not a worship service, I had no other frame of reference.

A priest is a priest, no matter where she happens to be. Her job is to recognize the holiness in things and hold them up to God. Her job is to speak in ways that help other people recognize the holiness in things too. For twenty years I had done that in churches, surrounded by ecclesiastical furniture, stained glass, sacred language, and congregational expectations that kept me ever mindful of my vocation. Now I was going to try working without a net, in a room that might yet become a sanctuary.

On the morning of my first class, I woke before dawn and pulled a green corduroy dress over my head, one of several I had bought that had no black in them. Looking in the mirror, I did not like the way my neck looked—too exposed, as if I were baring it for an ax. I tried buttoning the bodice all the way to the top, but then I looked too Puritan. Settling for one un-done button, I grabbed my briefcase and my coat and headed out the door to work.

My plan was to put a boom box in the room before the first students arrived so that they walked in to the sound of an Indian *bhakta* singing love songs to God. The hallway was deserted when I got there, which pleased me very much. The door to the class-room was locked, which did not. Since it was 7:40 in the morn-ing, no one who might have a key had arrived yet. Returning to my office, I called security. By the time the officer arrived, I was standing in the hallway with two dozen sleepy-looking college students, my unplugged boom box in my hand.

My heart beat at the base of my throat as I handed out syl-labi and made welcoming chatter. Several of the students in the back row already had their heads cradled in their arms while those nearer the front nursed huge thermos cups of cof-fee. Perhaps I could keep them awake by moving around a lot and varying the tone of my voice, I thought. Perhaps I could nab their attention with some riveting narrative in spite of the early hour. Such strategies came easily to me after years and

years of preaching, only I was missing all of my props. I set my
notes on a desk instead of a pulpit, standing in front of a
blackboard instead of a cross. Without my vestments, I knew
my knees were showing. It was a clergyperson's variation on
the nightmare in which you discover that you have gone out in
public with no clothes on.

I was no longer the rector of Grace-Calvary Episcopal
Church. I was Mrs. Taylor, the new religion teacher, with no
altar rail to separate me from my new flock. As I called each of
them by name, I realized that I had not only lost all my props,
I had also lost much of my vocabulary. Words such as *Let us pray*
were not going to work with this crowd any better than *our
Lord Jesus Christ. Eucharist, Lent,* and *liturgy* could all go into the
recycle bin along with *confirmation, collect,* and *diocese.* The great-
est and most surprising loss of all, however, was the plural pro-
noun *we.*

For twenty years I had used that word in community without thinking twice about it. On Sundays after the sermon, I
had led the congregation in saying the Nicene Creed. "We believe . . ." I had begun alone, but by the third word they were
all saying it in unison with me " . . . in one God, the Father, the
Almighty, maker of heaven and earth, of all that is, seen and
unseen."

"In peace, we pray to you, Lord God."

"Most merciful God, we confess that we have sinned against
you . . ."

"We celebrate the memorial of our redemption, O Father . . ."

"And now, as our Savior Christ has taught us, we are bold
to say . . ."

I had said these words so often that they were cemented in my consciousness like old Beatles songs, but when I said "we believe" on the first day of class, I saw a look pass over the face of a young man named Kamal that let me know my *we* was too small for him. Later I would learn that he was a Hindu from Sri Lanka who had lots of practice with pronouns snapping shut on him. On that first day, all I knew was that my language had left him out, so that his face became the icon I focused on as I learned to speak anew.

As I warmed to my topic that first Thursday morning, I found myself saying things that were not in my notes. I told the students that while they might think they were there to fulfill one of the general education requirements for gradua- tion, my class was going to give them a straight shot at making the world a better place. By learning more about what their neighbors held most sacred, they were going to be better equipped to love them, or at least slower to condemn them for conceiving God in a different way. In fifteen short weeks, they were going to feel less stupid about the rapidly changing coun- try in which they lived. They were going to know better than to step on their roommate's prayer rug or to order a ham-and- cheese sandwich at a kosher delicatessen. They were going to know how to tell the difference between a Greek Orthodox church and a Roman Catholic church just by looking, and they were going to know the name of the elephant-headed god be- hind the cash register at the Indian restaurant. They were going to understand why the First Amendment made the United States such an interesting place to live. They were going to be better citizens of the world.

With any luck, they were even going to be saddled with questions that would keep them awake at night, increasing both their awe before the mystery of life and their kinship with other mortals. I hoped they would like my class, I told them, but that was not my main concern. My main concern was their utter transformation. I wanted their education to change their lives, their dreams, and their futures. I wanted what they learned to call all their old certainties into question and enlarge the boundaries of their known worlds. I wanted them to discover how capable they were, how rich their imaginations were, and how much their choices mattered in the grand scheme of things.

As the students warmed to what I was saying, I discovered things that still worked even without props. The call to higher purpose still worked. The promise of greater understanding still worked, along with the live current that linked human beings. The more I gave to the students, the more they gave back. We rose to the occasion of one another's presence, and before the hour was over I knew that while the scenery had changed, my vocation had not. I was still on holy ground. All the familiar human sorrows were in that room, all the human hunger for meaning and for love. I was still in the privileged position of choosing words that fell into deep water, and of asking the kinds of questions that mattered. I would have to become better at charades, by which I mean I would have to act out virtues that I had once taken shortcuts through with words, but I was in a room full of eighteen- and nineteen-year-olds—a group of people most clergy see very little of in church—and until I said or did something incredibly stupid they seemed inclined to trust me.

When I dismissed them at 9:15, I registered all that I had lost: my congregational base, my liturgical language, my exquisite vestments, my clerical distinction. They were the same things I had wanted so badly to lose in the swimming pool that night of the lobster party. Watching them fall away from me now, I thought that they looked better on the blue bottom of the pool than they did on me. Breaking the surface at last, I saw that my humanity was all I had left to work with. I saw in fact that it was all I had ever had to work with, though it had never seemed enough.

There was no mastering divinity. My vocation was to love God and my neighbor, and that was something I could do any-where, with anyone, with or without a collar. My priesthood was not what I did but who I was. In this new light, nothing was wasted. All that had gone before was blessing, and all yet to come was more.

# PART THREE

# Keeping

*What we are all more or less lacking at this moment
is a new definition of holiness.*
PIERRE TEILHARD DE CHARDIN

In the twenty-first year of my priesthood, I empty the bag
of my old convictions on the kitchen table to decide what
I will keep. The clerical collar I once wore like a wimple is
brown where it has rubbed against my skin. My human dirt has
come off on it, and I have lost all will to bleach it clean. I wear
it very seldom now, both because the plastic band bites into my
neck and because it draws more attention than I want. I love
watching people, which becomes far more difficult when they
are watching me. Street clothes are good camouflage, and my
gray hair is enough to get me a seat on the subway without
changing the way people talk when they see me. Since I still
serve as a guest preacher some Sundays, I will keep the collar.
The neckline of my cassock does not stand up right without it,
and the jolt I receive when I see it in the mirror tells me that I
am not through with this mark of office yet.

The pectoral cross made from two old carpenter's nails is
still sharp enough to prick my hands. After I left church I
could not find it anywhere and thought I had lost it for good.
Then the same man who made it for me brought it back to me,

fished up from a crevice in the sacristy where I had dropped it. I am glad to have it back, although I have many more, which I liked to wear back when a cross meant only love to me. Now I know too many people who regard it as a weapon. Some have been cut deeply by it, not once but over and over again, while those who wield it like a rapier seem to believe that their swordplay pleases God. Either way, I find myself reaching for symbols with less violence in them.

The one I wear most often now is a silver circle with three waves curling toward each other in the center. Jesus is one of those waves, but he is not the only one. When his wave breaks, the Holy Spirit's wave picks up where his left off, and when the Holy Spirit's wave breaks, the water spills back toward the Wave Maker. The clerk who sold me this circle told me that it did not stand for anything, but I knew better. I knew I needed a symbol for the fullness of God, which cannot be reduced to any one name alone. While I wear the circle, I will keep the cross, even though I am not sure that the symbol can survive its abuse. For me, it is a reminder of Jesus's willingness to risk everything for the love of God's little ones. The cross he died on reminds me that his Way is not the way of violence against his enemies or victory over those who do not believe in him, but the way of self-annihilating love for God and neighbor.

Because this is such a difficult way, I can understand why some Christians see it as a kind of bluff on God's part—the temporary casting of Jesus in the role of a humble servant until the last act of the play, when he will return to the stage a mighty victor—but I cannot make any more sense out of "triumphant Christians" than I can out of "conquering servants" or "warrior babies." If Jesus meant for his followers to rule the world, then why did he teach them to wash feet? As difficult as it is to accept, I believe that his death on the cross reveals the God who suffers for love instead of punishing the unloving, the God who lays down his life for his friends. In the words of W. H. Vanstone, set to a hymn that never fails to bring tears to my eyes, "Here is God: no monarch he, throned in easy state to reign; here is God, whose arms of love, aching, spent, the world sustain."

I will keep the prayer book and hymnal in which this hymn is marked with a purple ribbon. Bound together in a single volume, these two books show the wear and tear of a thousand Sundays. A red ribbon marks the pages of the communion service, which have been handled so often that the corners are dark with fingerprints. The pages of the baptismal service are puckered from all the holy water that children have flung on them over the years, and the burial office too, from the rain that fell on them at the graveside service for a young mother. There is a yellow and red picture of a clown stuck in the pages of "Thanksgiving for a Child," drawn for me by a girl named Harriett who signed her name in block letters so that I would not forget her, as I have not, though she must have children of her own by now.

This volume is so worn that I have long meant to replace it, but I have grown too fond of it to do that now. I like the cracked cover, with almost all of the gold rubbed off the cross. I like the crumpled pages, which show their age. The looks of this book tell the truth about where I have been. Although I do not spend nearly as much time in its pages anymore, I value the time I spent there, along with the people who prayed and sang these pages with me. When I need prayers wiser than my own, I can still find them in this book. When I need to sing what I feel instead of saying it, I can still find songs here that lift up my heart.

Like my prayer book and hymnal, my small leather-bound Bible is limp from long use. In thirty years, I have barely made a dent in it, although I have spent the better part of those years mining its treasures. If you look at it from the side, you can discover my favorite places to dig: Exodus, Job, and Hosea in the first testament; Mark, Luke, and Acts in the second. Like most Christians, I have my own canon, in which I hear God speaking most directly to me, but I also like the parts in which God sounds like an alien, since those parts remind me that God does not belong to me. I do not pretend to read the Bible any more objectively than those who wrote it for me. To read it literally strikes me as a terrible refusal of their literary gifts.

I will keep the Bible, which remains the Word of God for me, but always the Word as heard by generations of human beings as flawed as I. As beautifully as these witnesses write, their divine inspiration can never be separated from their ardent desires; their genuine wish to serve God cannot be divorced from their self-interest. That God should use such blemished creatures to communicate God's reality so well makes the Bible its own kind of miracle, but I hope never to put the book ahead of the people whom the book calls me to love and serve.

I will keep the Bible as a field guide, which was never intended to be a substitute for the field. With the expert notes kept by those who have gone before me, I will keep hunting the Divine Presence in the world, helped as much by the notes they wrote in the margins while they were waiting for God to appear as by their astonished descriptions of what they saw when God did. I know that nine times out of ten, the truth scripture tells is the truth about the human search for God. Still, with the help of the guide, there is always the hope of glimpsing the bright dove that splits the sky, fluttering in full view before turning with a whirr and a cry to make its clean getaway.

IN HER BOOK on the art of personal narrative, Vivian Gornick says that it is everyone's inclination "to make of his own disability a universal truth."* I have tried not to do that, especially since I do not believe that it is possible to proclaim a universal truth about churches that remain so doggedly particular. Grace-Calvary is as rooted in rural north Georgia as the Appalachian Mountains are. When I travel to Boston, Minneapolis, or Los Angeles, I enter a religious landscape so different from my own that I need a translator in order to communicate.

I have also come to appreciate the first few chapters of the Revelation to John, in which the writer of that visionary book addresses the angels of seven churches in Asia Minor. Every church really does have its own angel, I think. Some of those

---

*The Situation and the Story* (New York: Farrar, Straus, Giroux, 2001), 135.

guardians are still burning brightly, while some have lost their tail feathers and others are dead though not yet buried. Sometimes all you have to do is walk through the door of a church and sniff the air to know which is which. When I was deciding whether to go to Grace-Calvary, an experienced friend of mine gave me his advice. "Be sure you like the people," Bill said; to which I would add, "Be sure the angel is alive."

If I had to name my disability, I would call it an unwillingness to fall. On the one hand, this is perfectly normal. I do not know anyone who likes to fall. But, on the other hand, this reluctance signals mistrust of the central truth of the Christian gospel: life springs from death, not only at the last but also in the many little deaths along the way. When everything you count on for protection has failed, the Divine Presence does not fail. The hands are still there — not promising to rescue, not promising to intervene — promising only to hold you no matter how far you fall. Ironically, those who try hardest not to fall learn this later than those who topple more easily. The ones who find their lives are the losers, while the winners come in last.

For most of my adult life, what I have wanted most to win is nearness to God. This led me to choose a vocation that marked me as God's person both in my eyes and in the eyes of others. I gave myself to the work the best way I knew how, which sometimes exhausted my parishioners as much as it exhausted me. I thought that being faithful meant always trying harder to live a holier life and calling them to do the same. I thought that it meant knowing everything I could about scripture and theology, showing up every time the church doors were open, and never saying no to anyone in need. I thought that it meant ignoring my own needs and those of my family until they went away altogether, leaving me free to serve God without any selfish desires to drag me down.

I thought that being faithful was about becoming someone other than who I was, in other words, and it was not until this project failed that I began to wonder if my human wholeness might be more useful to God than my exhausting goodness.

Several years ago now, I met a former parishioner in the city where he and his family moved so that he could accept a new job. We had gotten to know one another when we both worked in Christian education—he as the chair of the parish committee and I as the priest in charge. When we met again, he was the new president of an urban university and I had moved to Clarkesville. After we had filled each other in on our new lives, I asked him where he was going to church. With no hesitation, he said that he was not going anywhere. His life was full. His work was valuable. He spent his days with people of many faiths and no faith at all, who gave him ample opportunity to practice his own.

Still immersed in church life, I was skeptical. "Say more," I said.

"After a lot of listening," he said, "I think I finally heard the gospel. The good news of God in Christ is, 'You have everything you need to be human.' There is nothing outside of you that you still need—no approval from the authorities, no attendance at temple, no key truth hidden in the tenth chapter of some sacred book. In your life right now, God has given you everything that you need to be human."

After all these years, I have no doubt added to his words, but only because I have thought about them so often. While there are clearly many different ways to be human, and not all of them praiseworthy, it remains possible to see Jesus not as the founder of a new religion but as the exemplar of a new way of being human—a new Adam, in the language of the apostle Paul—who lived and died with such authentic faith in God that he gave his followers the courage to try to do the same thing. For obvious reasons, they could not sustain this alarming freedom for long, so they turned the faith of Jesus into the religion about Jesus and the rest is history. In a quip that makes the rounds, Jesus preached the coming of the kingdom, but it was the church that came.

All these years later, the way many of us are doing church is broken and we know it, even if we do not know what to do about it. We proclaim the priesthood of all believers while we continue living with hierarchical clergy, liturgy, and architecture. We follow a Lord who challenged the religious and political institutions of his time while we fund and defend our own. We speak and sing of divine transformation while we do everything in our power to maintain our equilibrium. If redeeming things continue to happen to us in spite of these deep contradictions in our life together, then I think that is because God is faithful even when we are not. When we are able to trust the gospel that our human love of God and one another is the sum total of what we were put on earth to do, and that we have everything we need to be human, then redeeming things will continue to happen, both because and in spite of us. They will happen because God loves life so much that even at the grave we make our song Alleluia, alleluia, alleluia.

Reynolds Price, who is one of my favorite novelists, now writes from a wheelchair because of a rare spinal cancer that almost killed him twenty years ago. His compelling book about that experience is called *A Whole New Life,* in which he evokes the healing vision of Jesus that he believes saved his life. While Price survived both the cancer and its cure, he was not able to avoid death altogether. "When you undergo huge traumas in middle life, everybody is in league with us to deny that the old life is ended," he said in an interview in the *Oxford Review.* "Everybody is trying to patch us up and get us back to who we were, when in fact what we need to be told is, You're dead. Who are you going to be tomorrow?"

This is the gospel truth, as true of the church as of her members. All the church has ever needed to rise from the dead is memory, bread, wine, and Holy Spirit — that, and care for the world that is at least equal to her care for her own preservation. Where church growth has eclipsed church depth, it is possible to hear very little about the world except as a rival for the human resources needed by the church for her own survival.

A friend of mine, who was for a time in charge of continuing education at a seminary in lower Manhattan, challenged this idea by reversing the usual polarity between the school and the city. Instead of inviting people to General Seminary to learn about God, Harry invited them to stay at General Seminary while they learned what God was doing in the city. After days on the streets and nights at the theater, the pilgrims returned to the seminary to process their encounters with the divine.

The clear message was that God did not live at the seminary. God lived in the world. The seminary existed so that people had a place to try and make sense of their experience in the world, as well as a community to support them while they did. In the seminary library, they could find helpful field guides written by earlier seekers. In the classroom, they could learn useful language for what they had experienced, along with tested methods for discerning what was life-giving from what was not. In the refectory, over second and third cups of coffee, they could hash out honorable ways to respond to what they had experienced, and, in the chapel, they could voice their gratefulness for all of this to God.

If churches saw their mission in the same way, there is no telling what might happen. What if people were invited to come tell what they already know of God instead of to learn what they are supposed to believe? What if they were blessed for what they are doing in the world instead of chastened for not doing more at church? What if church felt more like a way station than a destination? What if the church's job were to move people out the door instead of trying to keep them in, by convincing them that God needed them more in the world than in the church?

I may have left the house, but I have not left the relationship. After twenty years of serving Mother Church at the altar, I have pitched my tent in the yard, using much of what she taught me to make a way in the world. Perhaps I should have remained a deacon and never become a priest, but it is too late for that now. I prefer to think that I have been given another chance to be a priest, although with few of the assurances that attracted me before.

During my early years in parish ministry, I conceived of faith as the core certainty about God and godly things that equipped me for ministry. When people had questions about Jesus's divinity or the activity of the Holy Spirit, I had reasonable answers for them. When they wanted to know why terrible things happened to good people, I could at least introduce them to the language of theodicy.

Not until my father died did I feel my way into a different concept of faith. As many things as he and I talked about through the years, faith was not one of them. I knew that he had gone to Catholic school in Sioux Falls, where he remembered both the constraints placed on his curiosity and the cruelty of the nuns. After I was ordained, he told me hair-raising stories about how his mother made him miniature vestments when he was a boy so that he could play priest at a cardboard altar. When he was fifteen, he left home to get as far away from all of that as he could and ended up working in the San Francisco shipyards. Although he and my mother became confirmed in the Episcopal Church in their late fifties, I never knew whether that was because they believed in God or because they believed in me.

My father's demise was a slow one, during which he lost body parts to three kinds of cancer. The tumors in his brain were finally what killed him, but not without first robbing him of the mental keenness that had been his most prized faculty. Spoken words escaped him. He forgot how to spell. Finally, when he could no longer lift a spoon to his mouth, he suffered a seizure that landed him in the emergency room. Five days later he was admitted to Hospice Atlanta, where my family and I sat with him for the six days more that it took him to die.

He and I were past talking by then, which meant that I never found out where he was with God. All I found out was how helpless love can be, with nothing left to do but suffer alongside with the beloved. Marooned by my father's bed day after day, listening to him whimper in the night, unsure what he believed about God, unsure that it mattered, wanting to pray, for him and for me, without managing anything much beyond "Please," I discovered that faith did not have the least thing to do with certainty. Insofar as I had any faith at all, that faith consisted of trusting God in the face of my vastly painful ignorance, to gather up all the life in that room and do with it what God alone knew how to do.

Since then, I have learned to prize holy ignorance more highly than religious certainty and to seek companions who have arrived at the same place. We are a motley crew, distinguished not only by our inability to explain ourselves to those who are more certain of their beliefs than we are but in many cases by our distance from the centers of our faith communities as well. Like campers who have bonded over cook fires far from home, we remain grateful for the provisions that we have brought with us from those cupboards, but we also find them more delicious when we share them with one another under the stars.

This wilderness experience sets up a real dilemma for some of us, since we know how much we owe to the traditions that shaped us. We would not be who we are without them, and we continue to draw real sustenance from them, but insofar as those same traditions discourage us from being with one another, we cannot go home again. In one way or another, every one of us has gotten the message that God made us different that we might know one another, and that how we treat one another is the best expression of our beliefs.

When my father's older brother visited Clarkesville recently, I took him to visit Grace-Calvary Church. He had never seen it. I had not seen it for quite some time, but since the door is never locked I knew we would be welcome. Walking up the painted gray steps with my uncle, I could feel my heart grow larger in my chest, as if we had suddenly gained more altitude than we had. I tugged on the brass door handle and it opened, allowing us both inside the dollhouse church that I had fallen in love with before I ever met the people. The day must have been a Saturday, since I could smell the communion bread that someone had left in the sacristy—either that or it was Jesus, coming to me in the form that I had held in my hands so often. That smell alone was enough to tell me that I would never leave church, not really. I am too in need of the regular reminder that falling is the way of life. Where else do human beings recognize the bread of heaven in a broken body, or know that their lives depend on eating that food?

MANY YEARS AGO now, when I was invited to speak at a church gathering, my host said, "Tell us what is saving your life now." It was such a good question that I have made a practice of asking others to answer it even as I continue to answer it myself. Salvation is so much more than many of its proponents would have us believe. In the Bible, human beings experience God's salvation when peace ends war, when food follows famine, when health supplants sickness and freedom trumps oppression. *Salvation* is a word for the divine spaciousness that comes to human beings in all the tight places where their lives are at risk, regardless of how they got there or whether they know God's name. Sometimes it comes as an extended human hand and sometimes as a bolt from the blue, but either way it opens a door in what looked for all the world like a wall. This is the way of life, and God alone knows how it works.

Although we might use different words to describe it, most of us know what is killing us. For some it is the deadly rush of our lives; for others it is the inability to move. For some it is the prison of our possessions; for others the crushing poverty that dooms our children to more of the same. Few of us can choose our circumstances, but we can choose how we respond to them. To be saved is not only to recognize an alternative to the deadliness pressing down upon us but also to be able to act upon it. Even those who have no choice but to be carried toward safety on stretchers will eventually be given the chance take up their mats and walk, and even those whose legs still will not work can discover how agile a healed spirit can be.

On the twentieth anniversary of my ordination, I would have to say that at least one of the things that almost killed me was becoming a professional holy person. I am not sure that the deadliness was in the job as much as it was in the way I did it, but I now have higher regard than ever for clergy who are able to wear their mantles without mistaking the fabric for their own skin. As many years as I wanted to wear a clerical collar and as hard as I worked to get one, taking it off turned out to be as necessary for my salvation as putting it on. Being set apart was the only way I could learn how much I longed to be with everyone else. Being in charge was the only way I could learn how much I wanted to be in community.

Teaching school is saving my life now. While I am still in charge of my classroom, I am not God's designated representative in my students' lives. They can take me or leave me, and few need me to authorize their understanding of how the world works. Because we do not rely on one another for ultimate meaning, we are able to talk about things that might be too hot for us to handle if we were more dependent on one another. Our covenant exists on a syllabus, not in the Bible, which allows us to ask unorthodox questions of one another. Since we are in a classroom and not a church, we are free to wonder instead of to witness. Our answers change from day to day, as we too are changed by listening to one another. Compared to church, this may not be real community, but real transformation still happens in it.

Living in relationship with creation is saving my life now. I have lived so much of my life in relationship with ideas that the concrete realities of rain, drought, summer, and winter strike me with oracular force. Living off the land, I have discovered the organic connection not only between potatoes and dirt but also between honey and bees, ripe figs and fig wasps, boneless breasts and chickens, pine trees and paper mills. Paying attention to these things brings me back into my own body, which I tend to forget on a regular basis. Caring for animals helps me care for my own mute flesh, which in turn helps me understand what the Incarnation is all about. Matter matters to God.

Observing the Sabbath is saving my life now. For the first time in my life, I can rest without leaving home. With sundown on the Sabbath, I stop seeing the dust balls, the bills, and the laundry. They are still there, but they lose their power over me. One day each week I live as if all my work were done. I live as if the kingdom has come, and when I do the kingdom comes, for one day at least. Now, when I know the Sabbath is near, I can feel the anticipation bubbling up inside of me. Sabbath is no longer a good idea or even a spiritual discipline for me. It is my regular date with the Divine Presence that enlivens both body and soul.

Encountering God in other people is saving my life now. I do not look for angels anymore, although I have nothing against them. The clerk at the grocery store is messenger enough for me, at least if I give her a fraction of the attention that I lavish on my interior monologue. To emerge from my self-preoccupation long enough to acknowledge her human presence is no mean feat, but when I do I can almost always discover what she has to teach me—and not only she, but every person who crosses my path. While it is generally more pleasant for me to encounter people who support my view of reality, I am finding that people who see things otherwise tend to do me a lot more good. Like quantum physicists, they remind me that reality is more relational than absolute. Every time I am pretty sure that I have some absolute truth all worked out, a human being comes along to pose an exception to my rule. Over and over, the human exceptions prove to be more revelatory than the rules.

Committing myself to the task of becoming fully human is saving my life now. This is not the same as the job of being human, which came with my birth certificate. To become fully human is something extra, a conscious choice that not everyone makes. Based on my limited wisdom and experience, there is more than one way to do this. If I were a Buddhist, I might do it by taking the bodhisattva vow, and if I were a Jew, I might do it by following Torah. Because I am a Christian, I do it by imitating Christ, although I will be the first to admit that I want to stop about a day short of following him all the way.

In Luke's gospel, there comes a point when he turns around and says to the large crowd of those trailing after him, "Whoever comes to me and does not hate father and mother, wife and children, brothers and sisters, yes, and even life itself, cannot be my disciple" (14:26). Make of that what you will, but I think it was his way of telling them to go home. He did not need people to go to Jerusalem to die with him. He needed people to go back where they came from and live the kinds of lives that he had risked his own life to show them: lives of resisting the powers of death, of standing up for the little and the least, of turning cheeks and washing feet, of praying for enemies and loving the unlovable. That would be plenty hard enough for most of them.

If he could not shake the crowd off, they were all going to get themselves killed, or worse. They were going to venerate his path in place of finding their own. They were going to

expect him to tell them things that they could only discover
for themselves. So he turned around and said something guar-
anteed to discourage most of them from going any further. He
stopped the car so the spiritual hitchhikers could get out. Like
me, a lot of them decided that they did not have what it took
to be disciples after all. Drifting away in clumps of two and
three, they eventually found their ways back home, where they
started local chapters of the Friends of the Disciples, and to
everyone's great surprise that turned out to be enough. All
these years later, there are still a few who believe that becoming fully human is the highest honor they can pay to the incar-
nate one who showed them how.

Add this, then, to the list of things on the kitchen table that
I have decided I will keep: I will keep faith—in God, in God's
faith in me, and in all the companions whom God has given
me to help see the world as God sees it—so that together we
may find a way to realize the divine vision. If some of us do not
yet know who we are going to be tomorrow, then it is enough
for us to give thanks for today while we treat each other as well
as we know how. "Be kind," wrote Philo of Alexandria, "for everyone you meet is fighting a great battle." We may be in for a
long wait before the Holy Spirit shows us a new way to be the
church together, but in the meantime there is nothing to pre-
vent us from enjoying the breeze of those bright wings.


A COUPLE OF weeks ago, a stiff wind blew a homing pigeon
off course. I was just standing there in the garden when she
dropped from the sky with a whirr and looked at me as if I

should know what to do with her. I could see the orange band on her leg, but she would not let me catch her so I could read it. I was sure she would be on her way as soon as the weather improved, but instead she stuck around. For about two weeks she met me every afternoon for a little visit over cracked corn.

She was an entirely different kind of bird from the ones I was used to. She was not wounded, she was not tame, and she was not wild. She did not need me to take care of her. She left me no eggs. When the wild geese flew over, she and I both looked up at them. When the red-tailed hawk cried, we both gave a little start. For reasons beyond my understanding, she seemed to enjoy my company. For the same reasons, I enjoyed hers. She was a message I could not read, but she was sent to me nonetheless, and simply to see her seemed blessing enough.

Now the wind has taken her away again. At least I hope it was the wind and not a fox. The chickens and I are back to our daily routine, which is pleasant enough. Still, I cannot walk down to the garden without hoping to be startled by that descending commotion of beating wings and loose feathers, settling into something like a dove with a message for me. She came once, so I know she can come again.

I keep a handful of cracked corn in my pocket, just in case.

# Acknowledgments

I am first of all grateful to those who lived with me through the years covered in this book, beginning with the rector emeritus of All Saints' Church, Harry Pritchett, and my able associates at Grace-Calvary Church, Steve Lipscomb and Rob Wood. For my friends in both parishes who are too numerous to name, I offer thanks for teaching me what I know about being a priest, and for suffering my sometimes exhausting ministry with such grace. Thanks in particular to John Kollock for compiling the history of Grace Church found in Chapter 2 of this book, and to Bennett Sims, Frank Allan, and Neil Alexander for being such good bishops to me. I am grateful to Ray Cleere for giving me my job, to Tim Lytle for doing all the real work at Piedmont College for both of us, and to Tommy Mealer for making farm life both fun and possible.

I am also grateful to those who offered words of encouragement while this memoir was in the works, including Nora Gallagher, Diana Butler Bass, Rick Lischer, Deborah Botti, and Bill Brosend. Without the ready humor and steady support of Tom Grady, I would never have made it beyond my first draft

The team at Harper San Francisco took what I gave them and turned it into something much better. For all these good souls I offer hearty thanks.

Yale University, Furman University, Calvin College, *The Christian Century*, and Kanuga Conference Center all offered me early opportunities to explore the territory covered in these pages. Thanks to Jerry Streets, Elaine Nocks, Dale Brown, Jennifer Holberg, David Heim, Debra Bendis, and Susan Sloan for those invitations.

Finally, I acknowledge those nearest and dearest to me, many of whose names do not show up in this book although they have formed a circle around my heart for most of the years these pages describe. I bow low to Martha Sterne and Judy Barber. I remember my father, Earl, with fathomless love. I honor Grace, my own mother hen, to those same depths. I bless Katy and Jennifer, my prized sisters; Claire and Kathleen, my daughters by marriage and my friends by choice; and all the men and children whom these good women have brought into my life, namely, Dan, Mac, John, Hawley, Will, Maddie, Patrick, and Ava. As always, I end with thanks to Ed, for being my first and best reader as well as my heart's safe shelter and my most trusted friend. *Deo Gratias.*

*The Feast of Epiphany*

*2006*

# Recommended Reading

*Earthly Good* by Martha Sterne (Akron, Ohio: OSL Publications, 2003)

*The Good Book* by Peter J. Gomes (San Francisco: HarperSanFrancisco, 1996)

*The Heart of Christianity* by Marcus Borg (San Francisco: HarperSanFrancisco, 2003)

*A Hidden Wholeness* by Parker Palmer (San Francisco: Jossey-Bass, 2004)

*Learning to Fall* by Philip Simmons (New York: Bantam Books, 2000)

*Listening for the Heartbeat of God* by J. Philip Newell (New York: Paulist Press, 1997)

*Open Secrets* by Richard Lischer (New York: Broadway, 2001)

*The Sabbath* by Abraham Joshua Heschel (New York: Farrar, Straus and Giroux, 1975)

*Secrets in the Dark* by Frederick Buechner (San Francisco: HarperSanFrancisco, 2006)

*The Solace of Fierce Landscapes* by Belden Lane (New York: Oxford University Press, 1998)

*What Are People For?* by Wendell Berry (San Francisco: North Point Press, 1990)

*A Whole New Life* by Reynolds Price (New York: Athenaeum, 1994)

*The Wisdom of Insecurity* by Alan Watts (New York: Vintage Books, 1951)

*The Wisdom Way of Knowing* by Cynthia Bourgeault (San Francisco: Jossey-Bass, 2003)